Photo Perren-Barberini, Zermatt, Switzerland

UNDERSTANDABLE JUNG

The older I grow the more impressed I am by the frailty and uncertainty of our understanding, and all the more I take recourse to the simplicity of immediate experience so as not to lose contact with the essentials, namely the dominants which rule human experience throughout the millennium. . . . It is quite possible that we look at the world from the wrong side and that we might find the right answer by changing our point of view and looking at it from the other side, i.e., not from the outside, but from the inside.

(Jung 1960, p. 580)

UNDERSTANDABLE JUNG

The Personal Side of Jungian Psychology

Written and illustrated
by
Harry A. Wilmer

Chiron Publications
Wilmette, Illinois

Printed in the United States of America.

04 03 02 01 00 99 98 97 96 95   11 10 9 8 7 6 5 4 3 2

Edited by Siobhan Drummond and Paige Britt.
Book design by Kirk George Panikis.
Cover design by Julie Burleigh.

For permissions, see page 265.

Library of Congress Cataloging-in-Publication Data:
Wilmer, Harry A., 1917–
    Understandable Jung : the personal side of Jungian psychology / written and illustrated by Harry A. Wilmer.
      p. cm.
    Includes bibliographical references and index.
    ISBN 0–933029–69–1 : $18.95
    1. Psychotherapy.   2. Jung, C. G. (Carl Gustav), 1875–1961.
I. Title.
RC480.5.W493 1994
150.19'54—dc20   93–10581
                                                CIP

For Jim Wilmer

Table of Contents

Harry A. Wilmer

Harry A. Wilmer

Harry Wilmer is president, director, and founder of the Institute for the Humanities at Salado. He is a senior analyst in the Interregional Society of Jungian Analysts and member of the International Association for Analytical Psychology.

Wilmer received an M.D. and Ph.D. from the University of Minnesota. He received his psychiatric training at the Mayo Clinic, where he later became a staff member. After being trained as a Freudian analyst at the San Francisco Psychoanalytic Society, he took training in Jungian psychology in San Francisco and as a Guggenheim Fellow in Zürich.

Wilmer has held a National Research Council Fellowship in the Medical Sciences at Johns Hopkins University. He has been a professor of psychiatry at Stanford University, the University of California, San Francisco, and at the University of Texas Health Science Center, San Antonio.

He introduced the concept of therapeutic community in the United States, published in his *Social Psychiatry in Action.* This book was later made into the award-winning movie, *People Need People*, with Fred Astaire, Lee Marvin, and Arthur Kennedy playing Dr. Wilmer. It was later also produced as a play.

PBS documentaries on Dr. Wilmer's work include "Youth Drug Ward" on the Haight Ashbury drug scene, "The Common Eye" on art therapy, and "Facing Evil," a 90-minute documentary of the Salado Institute symposium, by Bill Moyers in his "World of Ideas" series.

Wilmer has published thirteen books and 190 scientific articles. His first book, written when he had tuberculosis in 1941, was a best-seller called *Huber the Tuber: Lives and Loves of a Tubercle Bacillus.* He is the author of *Practical Jung: Nuts and Bolts of Jungian Psychotherapy,* to which this volume forms a sequel.

Preface

My parents have a lovely antique wooden plaque in their home inscribed with a Latin phrase, *ad asper per ardua.* From adversity to the stars. I have often reflected upon and taken comfort in those words. They say so much, so simply. As this book says so much, so simply.

I have been interested in Jung for many years. I suggested to my father that he write a book that would explain, in accessible terms, the basics of Jungian psychology and describe what the process of analysis is all about. *Practical Jung* and now *Understandable Jung* are the outcome of that suggestion.

Jungian writing is often deep and ponderous. My father's creative illustrations and off-the-wall humor, along with his lively text, present Jungian ideas and concepts in an accessible and light-hearted manner. I think it is important that the notions of introspection and individuation reach a wide audience.

My experience with prejudice tells me that, in general, people have strong negative associations with individuals who see a counselor or therapist. At the most public level in America, we denounce individuals running for political office if it is uncovered that they have been to a psychiatrist! Do we really want people running the country who are blind to the self beneath the persona?

It is troubling that individuals receive scorn for looking within, for seeking to understand their psyches, and for working to improve the quality of their inner life. If we do not understand ourselves, it becomes impossible to understand and accept others, especially those who are different from us.

My father has helped guide many individuals on their journey "from adversity to the stars," and in this book he shares with us many of his reflections and insights. *Understandable Jung* will give those who are new to Jung a glimpse into the world of Jung. And, to those who "know" Jung, it offers new, creative ways of looking at familiar concepts.

—Mary Wilmer

Introduction

We are wiser than we know. Emerson, 1841

Shall we begin with gods and goddesses, mandalas, minotaurs, and alchemy, with quaternities and coniunctionis, and that sort of thing?

Not by a long shot.

With mysticism and the I Ching?

Of course not.

To understand Jungian psychology, it is best to begin with simple ideas, of which there are a great many, and then on to more complex concepts that are understandable to the ordinary intelligent person. Many people have been turned off by analytical psychology, which is what Jung called his work, partly because they don't read his original volumes, which, it is fair to say, don't read easily. Many individuals are turned off by Jungian psychology because it sometimes breeds cultist groups. Blind belief in the tarot cards and astrology, adoration of the Kundalini White Serpent and the chakras enshrine Jung in chimera glitz.

Understandable Jung is an attempt to present Jung's ideas (both simple and deep) in clear language through sketches I have made, images, photographs, and cartoons of the humorous side of our deep psyches.

A word about the nature of the dialogues that I use in this book. The "other" with whom I dialogue is usually my image of the skeptical reader, a person who challenges me and forces me to be clear, stick to the point, and not fall victim to the very things that I am warning about. Sometimes this voice is a man, sometimes a woman, and sometimes a child. I do not always like the "other," but then the "other" does not always like me. It would be a mistake for the reader to imagine that this is the way I usually talk to myself while I am working with a patient or a student or friend. I am actually quite kind in my inner dialogue with myself, and yet from time to time I do harshly bring myself up straight if my mind wanders or if I am being too sympathetic instead of empathetic. Basically, in this book I am talking with my imagined reader—you.

This book addresses the personal side of Jungian psychology based on my personal participation in the act of understanding. Large portions of this book address dreams, which are perhaps the most personal expression of the psyche. In remembering and telling of dreams, as well as listening to and searching for meaning in dreams, one is enmeshed in the personalities of both the dreamer and the listener. Jung remarked that each school of psychology is a personal confession. So is this book a confession of my commitment to personal understanding. Its form, format, and images are approximations on the way to understanding and clarifying Jungian psychology.

If You Think I Am Defending and Defining Jungian Hypotheses, You Are Wrong. I Am Reporting My Experience With Them.

There is no doubt that we must have hypotheses
to think for ourselves and talk with others.
That Jung expressed his hypotheses—
Anima and Animus, Shadow and Self, etc.—
as useful ideas for understanding human relationships
implies that that is how we may use them.

You might prefer bright, shiny, nascent ideas and
set your own hypotheses in the forefront.
I prefer to present the shoulders of the giant
on which I stand to see afar,
not because they are the absolute best or only shoulders,
but because experience has taught me how
extraordinarily useful they are to me
in enlightening and creating insight and empathy.
We all come up with different facts of experience.
Jung said we would and gave three cheers for that
eventuality.

Alfred Jules Ayer wrote in *Language, Truth & Logic:*

> It appears, then, that the "facts of experience" can never compel us
> to abandon a hypothesis. A man can always sustain his convictions
> in the face of apparently hostile evidence if he is prepared to make
> the necessary "ad hoc" assumptions. But although any particular
> instance in which a cherished hypothesis appears to be refuted can
> always be explained away, there must remain the possibility that the
> hypothesis will ultimately be abandoned. Otherwise it is not a
> genuine hypothesis. For a proposition whose validity we are
> resolved to maintain in the face of any experience is not a hypothe-
> sis at all, but a definition. In other words, is not a synthetic but an
> analytic proposition. (1946, p. 95)

It is in this spirit
that I will not indulge
in the challenges and refutations, the doubts
and the outrages, but will stick
to the things that are, in my mind at least,
uniquely in the realm of analytical psychology.

"This, too, shall pass."
For now, however, cheers and right on.

Acknowledgments

Paige Britt, the associate editor of the Institute for the Humanities, performed an enormous task in editing this manuscript.

I am grateful to Murray Stein at Chiron Publications for urging me to write this book and his patience in waiting for three years for me to deliver it to him. It has also been good to be able to work with Siobhan Drummond, managing editor of Chiron.

My wife, Jane, is acknowledged with love for her encouragement and affirmation.

My daughter, Mary, who has written the preface, first asked me to write *Practical Jung* and then this sequel.

This book has gone through so many rewrites that it is only appropriate to acknowledge my faithful word processor.

—Harry Wilmer

PART

ONE

Why I Became a Psychoanalyst and Therapist

Shock day at the Rochester (Minn.) State Hospital, 1947: Patients were lined up in all the beds in the ward. The doctor moved down the line with the machine, and as the doctor administered the electroshocks one by one—without sedation—the nurses held down the patients to decrease the number of fractures. Today, both muscle relaxants and anesthesia are used.

The scene in 1947 was ghastly.

Dr. Walter Freeman had introduced lobotomy. He gave a demonstration at the Rochester State Hospital and said that he had already performed about 5,000 of them. The lobotomy was called the "ice pick" procedure because its main instrument looked just like an ice pick. With the patient sitting in a chair—again no anesthesia—Dr. Freeman punched the instrument just above the eyeball into the skull and, with a sweeping motion, severed the connections behind the frontal cortex. It stopped the wild behavior of schizophrenics, but left the patient like a zombie.

I found this procedure gruesome.

In 1955, I was assigned to an insulin treatment ward for schizophrenic patients. The treatment consisted of using insulin to induce coma in these patients. Some died. It was terrifying to me. Years later, in the Veterans Administration, long after insulin coma was abandoned, I saw endless lines of schizophrenic patients who were walking automatons, drugged by huge doses of neuroleptic drugs. Some were kept on these doses for years—some as long as they lived. More than a few developed uncontrollable motor gestures such as facial grimaces and repetitive protrusion of their tongues—all untreatable (tardive dyskinesia).

In private sanitariums I saw patients restrained for long periods of time in leather cuffs or wrapped tightly in wet sheets that encompassed their bodies and arms (camisole). Others were laced into warm tub baths for hours under canvas covers.

Once I finally had an opportunity to direct my own ward in a naval psychiatric hospital, it is little wonder that I developed a therapeutic community in which no restraints were ever used and in which I never secluded a patient in a quiet room. This was no act of heroism. It was motivated by the fact that I could not bear to see secluded patients locked and drugged in "quiet rooms." About twenty percent of the patients received neuroleptic medication in moderate doses. Group therapy was the psychological treatment.

And there it began.

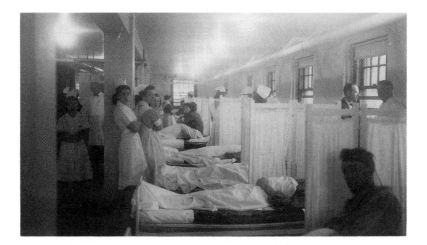

Shock day at Rochester State Hospital

Being Your Own Person

I always marveled at my Jungian analyst, his keen attention, his sharp look, his seemingly never-wavering attention, his strong silences and clear, straight messages. I wondered, would I ever be able to hold my attention so keenly and not let my mind wander? Or was I merely caught in too positive a transference? As years have passed and I, too, have really learned to listen, I marvel at my own attentiveness and almost unwavering listening, following my inner dialogue from clue to clue. I know it is possible to acquire the listening skill, because for years my mind wandered although I was never inattentive. So! It is possible to learn how to listen. It is a discipline.

And to look.

There was no way to know just how sharp my Freudian analyst was because he was invisible in his chair behind the couch. Was he asleep? Was he watching? Was he daydreaming? How could I tell if I couldn't see his eyes? And how could he know if he couldn't look into my eyes? And what kind of a foreshortened body lay in front of him? I know. In those days, I, too, sat behind the couch and saw this strange perspective laid out before me.

And the patient plays his hand. . . . Even if the analyst didn't look cautious and guarded, I could see an inner shadow person, cool and skeptical.

My professor of the history of medicine and anatomy, Richard Scammon (who had been dean of medical sciences at the University of Chicago and the University of Minnesota, and with whom I took a graduate degree), once told me, "There are few times in life that you can afford to prove that you are right. Choose them carefully."

Sooner or Later, You Will Have to Be Your Own Analyst

A Personal Experience:
As my Jungian analysis came to an end,
a very interesting thing happened.

I related a dream
and enthusiastically told my analyst
what I thought it meant—
                    expecting a response.

He would say something like, "You're right" or "You have it"
or he would just grunt.

I had said something quite good, I mused—
          a novel twist,
          a unique idea, maybe even
          an extraordinary interpretation.

But nothing happened.
There was a "lucid stillness."*

Three words kept spinning in my mind:
          "You have it."
Yes, that was all:
          "You have it."

What a disappointment!
          Goddamn it!

The Wise Old One didn't have one secret,
one mysterious wonderful word to add to
          "You have it."

---

*T. S. Eliot, quoted from Roget's International Thesaurus, 4th ed. (New York: Harper and Row, 1977), p. 337.

His words seemed to welcome a
Wise Old Man within me,
who after long gestation was coming out.

        There was silence
        as if a door
        had been gently
        closed. And I
        held a key.
   "You have it."

Poof! Even though he sat there looking at me,
he was not there as before.

      I could hear breathing.

For a split second, it was as if we were the same person,
and in that instant, he seemed suddenly to move
farther away than ever he had been.

The Wise Old Man I had been talking to
had become myself—wise man, old fool.

On the Art of Plain Speaking

Or How to Master Jungian Psychology by Just Learning Seventeen Words in One Minute

Whenever there are four of anything,
    Say: **Quaternity.**
Are you troubled? No wonder,
    You are in a **Complex.**
From time to time, when you don't understand,
    Say: **Enantiodromia**
And you will immediately feel much better,
    Even if you feel **Alchemical.**

Whenever there is a stranger lurking anywhere,
    Always whisper: **The Shadow.**
If the lights go out,
    Remember the **Collective Unconscious.**
If the lights come on,
    Cry out in joy: **Numinosum!**
Whenever you sense a mysterious woman,
    Behold the **Goddess.**

At every intersection at the crossroads of your life,
    You have arrived at the **Archetypal Junction.**
If you wonder who directs the traffic miracles,
    Look and behold the **Transcendent Function.**
Be careful where you say **Anima** or **Animus,**
    Because people make such gender fusses.
If you sink into the awful murk of despair, cheers!
    There dwells the **Two-Million-Year-Old Wise Man** (ah . . . Woman)

Time and again you will come to one of life's road blocks,
    The magic password is **Inner-Outer-Outer-Inner.**
And when you doodle, daddle, scribble and scramble,
    Do them in shades of **Mandalas.**
And if you feel intimidated by very awesome Jungians,
    Say: *Puer!* **to all those Circumambulators.**

Post-Jungianism

Some people find it fashionable to use the terms *post-Jungian* and *post-Jungians.*

For example, Andrew Samuels says:

> Nevertheless, the debt to Jung, to the "first generation of Jungians," and to the Classical School should not bind us to the shift in overall point of view, or vertex, that has been taking place in analytical psychology for the past twenty-five years. The post-Jungian vertex refers to an emotional involvement in the debates it evokes. I mean that if one or more of the debates within analytical psychology seems significant to you, then you are post-Jungian. Different opinions define the field.
>
> (1990, p. 294)

I do not understand that. It does not make sense to me. It seems to say that if some debate seems significant to you, then you can call yourself post-Jungian if you think obtaining such a description is an achievement. Just what does the designation "post-Jungian" suggest, though? Since everything after Jung is after Jung, how do you pin down the nefarious *point in time* that demarcates it as the post? Is it the hour Jung died or the imaginary twenty-five-year span? There is no such thing as a *point in time* except an arbitrary assumption that time stood still at some "instant" when it could be a point. Post-Jungianism began with political rhetoric and should remain there.

Let us delve deeper into the post-Jungian idea. For example, the same author of the above quote wrote:

> You will gather from these remarks that post-Jungian psychology is part of a poststructural matrix or, rather, that when I employ the term "post-Jungian," I am deconstructing analytical psychology. The key terms now are interaction—of psychic themes, patterns, images, emotions, instincts; and relativity—archetypes in the eye of the beholder, a dethroned self, and democratic individuation. *En passant* everything I have been saying applies clinically: microscopic examination of transference-countertransference interactions and befriending the image in all its particularity and specificity are both reactions to the same deficiencies in classical Jungian clinical technique.
>
> (Samuels 1990, p. 295)

Understandable Jung (*U.J.*) interviewed an analyst for his reactions:

U.J.: Can you explain the above quote on post-Jungian ideas to me?

ANALYST: Well, I guess he is saying that anything after Jung is *ipso facto*. I thought everybody knew that.

U.J.: But is that a poststructural deconstruction?

ANALYST: Beats me.

U.J.: Let me ask it another way, appealing to you as a former pathologist. What does it mean to have a microscopic examination of transference-countertransference?

ANALYST: Clinically, I would say that a microscopic examination of transference-countertransference suggests an archetype in the eye of the beholder or a dethroned self under a high-power microscope, democratic individuation under an oil-immersion microscope, and befriended images under an electron microscope.

U.J.: Can it be said that Jung planted a garden, which when it grew included various mutant, evolving, and withering offspring as well as some unanticipated developments and discoveries?

ANALYST: Yes.

U.J.: Before we conclude this interview, I would like to refer to the book from which the above quotations were taken. It is called, *C. G. Jung and the Humanities: Toward a Hermeneutics of Culture.* Hermeneutics is the study of methodological principles of interpretation and explanation. Can you simplify that for our readers?

ANALYST: In hermeneutics, one analyzes the methods of responding to patients with special psychological help as when "people go for help." My book *Practical Jung*, with its nuts and bolts, does this.

U.J.: Let me read what the hermeneutics book says in its preface. I am not detracting from a basically fine book, I am just pointing out some of its window dressing. The editors say:

Consequently, a properly Jungian hermeneutics involves the deployment of a flexible (pluralistic), comparative, and interdisciplinary "exegesis" that seeks out interpretative possibilities—not conclusions—and whose canonic procedures amplify the symbol-text by adding to it a wealth of personal and collective, historical and cultural analogies, correspondences, and parallels. In other words, the Jungian interpretation unfolds as a production—a positing of meanings *in relation to* and not the uncovering of *the meaning,* as in the Freudian operation—thereby advancing the genesis of meaning, collaborating in the genesis of the hermeneutic secret.

(Barnaby and D'Acierno 1990, p. xvii)

U.J.: What do you think about that?

ANALYST: You want what I think and not what I feel. I think that it is two sentences that contain ninety words.

U.J.: I mean, what do you think about the meaning, the interpretation, the explanation, the Jungian hermeneutic?!

ANALYST: Beats me.

U.J.: But clinically?

ANALYST: When I am with a patient, I have to keep my mind clear and sharp. When I try to speak in plain English, I don't remember ever exegesising.

U.J.: Please try to be more helpful. I am trying to understand the post-Jungian world.

ANALYST: Me, too.

U.J.: Thank you very much for your enlightening interview.

Because of this conceptual hair-splitting everybody is both right and wrong. . . . From such discussions we see what awaits me once I have become posthumous. Then everything that was once fire and wind will be bottled in spirit and reduced to dead nostrums. Thus are the gods interred in gold and marble and ordinary mortals like me in paper.

(Jung 1958, p. 469)

I can easily understand *posthumous Jung* as all that followed after June 6, 1961—the date of Jung's death. Any other post-Jungian designation (for example, what followed after the so-called first-generation Jungians) is arbitrary designation and therefore makes only arbitrary and arguable sense. The fact is, the separation between Jungian and post-Jungian that exists because a date was set is a separation only in the minds of those who set the date. And why, one may ask, is it in anyone's mind at all? In other words, it becomes "conceptual hair-splitting" of bottled fire and wind, interred in papers.

Jung disliked the idea of people being called "Jungians" and once said something along the lines of "I'm glad I'm Jung and not a Jungian" (1946, p. 405). I found it distasteful, when I was a Freudian, to call myself a Freudian, since it implied an allegiance to a man and not a body of thought. And there was a strange deification of Freud by my colleagues. I find it no less troublesome to call myself a "Jungian," since it implies that same discipleship idea. Nonetheless, for practical purposes, I use the term for lack of a better one.

In a sense, I have been doing something post-Jungian in this celebration of the body in its literal, untransformed state. My claim is that untransformation, literalness, tangible physical motion are all required before transformation becomes a possibility. Metaphor can go too far, become stuck and defensive—even literal! Maybe it is time to consider whether the Jungian stress on metaphoric *transformation* might have become, first, a consummation devoutly to be wished, perhaps a badge of honor, then an addiction, and finally a restrictive moral preoccupation sometimes encapsulated by uterine associations as a "feminine" capacity.*

So she went into the garden to cut a cabbage leaf, to make an apple pie; and at the same time a great she-bear, coming up the street, pops its head into the shop. "What! No soap?" So he died, and she very impudently married the barber; and there were present the Picaninnies, and the Joblillies, and the Garyalies, and the grand Panjandrum himself, with the round bottom at top, and they all fell to playing the game of catch as catch can, till the gun powder ran out at the heels of their boots.**

---

*Samuels 1990, pp. 304–305.
**Foote 1854, p. 516. Composed to test the vaunted memory of actor Charles Macklin.

Please Post

Announcement: Post Jungian Society Meeting.
Three Postmeridian, Brahman Hall, Newfoundland.
Post-Freudians and Postmasters Welcome.

Society Creed:
Droll allegiance to the Old Masters,
Apes of the Origin of Our Species,
From whom we have evolved into
Higher Beings.

In the pursuit of Individuation
With the proper *rites de sortie*
From the Postmodern Deconstructionists
We acknowledge that Time Indeed Doth Pass.

When Post Jungians are asked,
"Is Jungian analysis dead?"
We shall reply with proper solemnity,
"Is Offal Dead Right?"

And we shall sing,
      "There is no Post which is not Post Something,
                            Halleluiah!
      Nor any Prior which is not prior to what it is Prior to,
                            Hosanna!"

In the name of all honorable Post Wholes,
Post Docs, Post Hocs, and Postulants
We chant,
      "From Post to Post we cometh.
      And Post to Post we returneth.
      Cheers and Soliloquizes
      Til the Post Post Arriveth.
            Praise Be!"

Aria from the Operetta "On an Academic Toadstool"

She said that she was suffering from
an **overload of empathy.**
They say we are suffering from
compassion fatigue.

The opening bars of the OXYMORON OPERETTA:
O my empathy:
    'tis too much—too great a burden.
O my empathy:
    the great misnomer I overempathize.
Compassion. Compassion. I grow weary.
I am a dispassionate, compassionate exhaust pipe.
    Compassion in. Compassion out.
I am a drained drain, still a'draining.

Nothing Never Happens: like *excess empathy.*
Nothing Never Happens: like *compassion fatigue.*
    Except in their True Believers.

One cannot ever even be empathetic enough:
One can only be too sympathic, too giving,
and too self-conscious of what one mistakes for empathy.
To be empathic is always compassionate.
Neither can you have too much—only not enough.
To be burned out and overloaded with virtue
   is no virtue at all, but sham.
No one feels they are too rich. O the poor, poor.
O my sham, my dear old sham recitative: dear dear
Children of Sham, play "thank you" more and more.
O my sham, my dear old sham libretto! Sing ye
People of Sham: Rally around the flag
and sing the Sad Lullaby:
    "Thee Compassion Fugue Fatigue
    in Ye Flat Empathy."
                fini

Give and it shall be given unto you. Luke 6:48.
And the greatest of these is charity—caritas. I Cor. 13:13
Cast thy bread upon the water: for thou shalt find it after many days.
Eccles. 11:1

Empathy: The capacity to be within the other as the other is, not as you would be there, and at the same time to be separate. If you are too much in the other, you have given yourself up, and have no perspective and cannot love yourself as you would love your neighbor because you have cast yourself away in chimerical love. **Sympathy:** fellow-feeling for the other, and too much sympathy is overwhelming and no gift at all, but a chain. Thus, there is pity and contempt for the other and therefore for yourself.

On Being on a Spot

A RULE OF THUMB: The Only Spot You Are on Is the One on Which You Are Standing

For sure we all are on the proverbial spot from time to time.
But to bemoan that you are on the spot
is to forget how you got there
and why you are standing there now.

Admittedly, once on the spot,
other significant people are in a new
relationship in accordance with your position.
But being on the spot
may be just exactly where you should be standing.

Being there may make you feel vulnerable
or powerful as if you were king or queen of the hill,
but just remember the second rule.

ANOTHER RULE OF THUMB: Everybody Is Standing Somewhere on a Spot

The spot may demand *action, no action,* or *action in inaction* (according to the Tao principle of *wu wei,** literally "not doing").
I will give you an example of this phenomenon.

A Spot Story

In 1978, after working with Vietnam veterans at the Audie Murphy Veterans Administration Hospital in San Antonio for a number of years, it became obvious to me that nightmares and post-traumatic stress following catastrophic trauma were urgent and neglected missions of the VA. I managed to persuade the chief of staff to give me two years of sabbatical leave from ordinary VA duties to undertake a study of the nightmares of Vietnam combat veterans.

---

*Action in inaction, or *wu wei,* does not mean to avoid all action but rather all hostile or aggressive action. Many kinds of action are innocent. According to the Tao, even the use of military force may be committed with such an attitude that it perfectly exemplifies *wu wei.* According to Taoism of ancient China, virtuousness or nonconformity can be as aggressive as insults or silence (Welch 1966, p. 33).

I planned my project carefully. It was successful. However, this study did not endear me to my psychiatric colleagues in the VA because eventually it was a challenge to the traditional and ineffective, often destructive, treatment programs for Vietnam veterans at that time. Having received support from the chief of staff and the hospital director, and the grudging compliance from the psychiatric chief of staff, I nevertheless soon found the bureaucracy closing in. My secretary disappeared—reassigned to someone else. One Monday, I came to work to find that everything in my office had been boxed up and moved to a smaller office with a tiny window. Of course, the veterans kept coming to see me. I spent much time with each one and, where indicated, saw them in psychotherapy and a few in analysis. Most of them improved. They projected much good onto me, which did not please my overworked psychiatric peers, doggedly following the routines of the VA bureaucracy. As long as you play along, without ruffling feathers, you can work from 8 a.m. to 4:30 p.m. and go home for a drink. It wasn't that way with the spot on which I chose to stand.

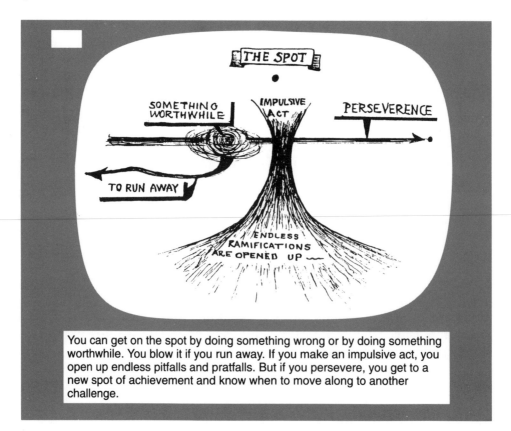

You can get on the spot by doing something wrong or by doing something worthwhile. You blow it if you run away. If you make an impulsive act, you open up endless pitfalls and pratfalls. But if you persevere, you get to a new spot of achievement and know when to move along to another challenge.

Therefore, I was on **the proverbial spot**. There were alternatives: I could persevere, convinced as I was that this was the right treatment. I could adapt my investigation to the VA treatment system. Or I could opt out of the whole endeavor.

I was a tenured professor at the university and didn't need the VA. I was also a psychoanalyst who could do well in private practice. Or I could act impulsively, take my complaint to Washington, talk to the newspaper reporters who, hearing of my work, came to see me. I could allow the patients to carry their complaints to the front office. I didn't do any of these things.

After all, they couldn't really hurt me, although they tried in ways I shall not recount.

In the end, I finished the project and was a survivor like my vets. Moreover, I learned about dreams to a depth that I had never even imagined. I helped 109 combat Vietnam veterans with PTSD, post-traumatic stress disorder, a diagnosis that was not yet officially accepted at that time.

The old Jungian principle of good coming out of bad, of the helpful side of the shadow, finding a center within, a connection with the Self, was strong enough to endure the pain that is inevitably associated with working psychologically with people who suffer from the effects of catastrophic trauma, be it war, accident, natural disaster, rape, violence, or torture.

PART

TWO

EVERYONE HAS A SHADOW

The bigger the person the bigger the shadow.

The Unconscious Is More Often Your Ally Than Your Enemy

We generally accept that we are not as much in control of our lives and own behavior as we think we are. The so-called self-made man becomes what he is through a myriad of people, things, and events. Yet these outside influences are not what control us; basically, we are at the mercy of our unconscious. It is hard to realize that the unconscious can be both our best friend and our worst enemy.

For the most part, we are not aware of these unconscious powers that evoke our feelings and reactions—especially the irrational ones that we consider out of character for the person we are convinced we are.

Something happens—someone says or does something—and we fall into deep anger, fear, or rage. We are helplessly in love—discover murderous fantasies and an unsuspected meanness. We can be and act out any of those "things" that possess us.

An emotional storm hits you with prejudice, envy, fear, hate, infatuation, resentment, wish for revenge, and tremendous tension. *The concatenation of feelings that drive you . . . that rationalized irrationality . . . is a clue that the archetype is stirring like a monster within.*

Well, it would help if you could be more specific.

Everyone experiences this spectrum of reactions and feelings within a family. Some people spend their whole lives blaming their mothers or their fathers (or both) for their life predicament. We find ourselves caught up in waves of recrimination, furious at people we trusted who betrayed our trust. Then we begin living according to the misery and suffering we blame on others. Those who might have loved us turn away and resent us.

Then we watch ourselves behaving toward our children just as we remember our parents treating us. So . . . is that the power of the unconscious? Then how can the unconscious be our dear friend and ally?

Yeah! How? How?

We all like to think of ourselves as totally conscious.
Then we don't understand why strange things creep into our lives and nightmares and frighten us.
Nightmares and strange forbidding things can be our allies.

Nightmares are unwelcome visitors that bring us dark news.
They reveal what we don't want to see.
They are messages from both the underworld of darkness
and the world of light and divinity.

We might consciously deny the darkness of our souls,
our thoughts and impulses,
but there is no amnesia in the unconscious.

**But how in the world can that help? I think we should not burden our minds
with all that garbage. So why must we be reminded of it in our nightmares?**

We must be reminded because forgetting begins with remembering
as it really was, not as we want to think it was
or as we are compulsively driven to remember it.
The nightmare calls us as witnesses to ourselves,
to balance our one-sided consciousness.

Tell me how!

Well, a person who leads an exemplary life outwardly—
who is seen as loving, giving, warm, caring, and remarkable—
may in a hidden life be the very opposite.
The preacher, the doctor, the philosopher, the analyst,
the lover, the spouse, or the parent,
whom everyone thinks is so wonderful
is seen in the intimacy of life as a miserable scoundrel,
mean, even cruel and sinister. How many people marry
only to find they married someone different from the person
with whom they thought they fell in love?
They are both the same!
The big persona hid the bad shadow.

Oh. I see.

Such a person will almost never take the bald truth from the
spouse or lover and will try to deny the obvious in dreams.
Like Scrooge's visits from the ghost of Marley
in Dickens's *A Christmas Carol,*
sooner or later the truth will come out.
The universal appeal of that story is evidence
of its archetypal legendary basis. Dream or vision,
the unconscious tells us like it is—*in spades.*
It pulls no punches when it is necessary to hit home.
Jung called this function of the dream *compensation.*
The dream compensates for the conscious blindness.
It reveals the shadow when one is inflated,
and it reveals goodness when one is deflated.
It is well known that people who live exemplary lives
sometimes run amok. Others ask in bewilderment,

"How could such a fine person do such evil things?"
They are filled with disbelief about what is as plain
as the noses on their faces.

Is this one reason why people scoff at psychology, psychiatry, psychotherapy, and analysis?

One reason they scoff is that the psychologically aware person
seems to carry dangerous ideas that threaten
purely rational people, or just ordinary people
who don't want to know anything unpleasant that they can avoid.
You would think that in the hedonistic, narcissistic, avaricious
times in which we live, when material wealth and possessions
are enshrined in our lives,
there would be less interest in the shadow.
Like being intoxicated, we would be numb to the shadow.
But the opposite is true. We are hooked on evil, meanness,
genocide, terrorism, nastiness. We are witnessing
so much child abuse and cruelty, rape, exploitation
of minorities, and murder. At the same time,
the highest order of spiritual and noble thought and writing
pours out endlessly. Why is this?
It is *because* we are out of balance
and have not learned to tolerate and reconcile opposites.

That is where Jungian psychology has much to offer.
It is a psychology of opposites and a way toward balancing
and centering. *Archetypes* are not images
of just one value but each is revealed to have opposite extremes.
For example, the Great Mother Goddess can be All Loving
as well as Devouring and All Consuming. We may pay homage
to the image of Mother or Father, but we all know
mothers and fathers who destroy their children's lives.

It is easy to scoff at psychology and psychiatry,
and admittedly there is a lot at which to scoff,
but the archetype of the Healer has also its opposites.
The fact that there are bad helpers
does not discredit the helping profession.

My friend says that Jung is particularly important in our contemporary world when we have deified science, when technology and statistics rule the roost. My friend says that all the more do we need to value the irrational and what defies logic.

Your friend is right.

As a matter of fact, all discovery begins with heresy,
from defying conventional logic and reason.
It is the unsuspected that overthrows
what in the past we enshrined as The Truth.
We are in danger of being destroyed by our science and technology
and are all the more desperately in need of the human spirit,
of the arts and humanities; we need to join the
"Two Cultures"—science and the humanities.
The gulf between them grows.

C. P. Snow writes:

> Literary intellectual at one pole—at the other scientists, and as the most representative, the physical scientists. Between the two a gulf of mutual incomprehension—sometimes (particularly among the young) hostility and dislike, but most of all lack of understanding. They have a curious distorted image of each other. (1959, p. 4)

Jung himself always valued the rational mind of science
as much as the mind of the analyst not bound to logic.
The growing interest in Jung reflects our cultural and spiritual needs.
Jungian psychology strives for an appreciation of balance
without ever disavowing the odd, or ignoring
the exception that does not prove the rule.

What about this opposite business? How does that affect me?

Well, if you get too high, you will fall to a low.
It is predictable. The high-flying are always going to crash.
What goes up comes down as sure as a gas balloon—
and for the same reason—elation and inflation.
The "hero" or star who experiences a meteoric rise,
faces the danger of the hubris. If we would pay attention
to our dreams, we might learn a thing or two.
Depression also serves a purpose:
the inner world demands a hearing. It pulls one down

to keep one from going up. But I do not favor depression
as a good thing, any more than a fever is healthy.
It is rather an unmistakable symptom of trouble in the psyche.

**But people are talking about "chemical imbalance" and treating depression
with drugs rather than listening and talking and psychotherapy. Isn't Jungian
psychology old hat?**

Only its misuse is to be discarded and judged harshly.
There is no doubt that the new antidepressant drugs
have therapeutic value, nor that some depressions
have a biological basis with origins in the brain.
But these facts do not touch our humanity
or how we perpetuate and foster depression ourselves.
Not all depressed people need drugs, and not all need
psychotherapy. It is now apparent that without psychotherapy,
however, drugs may only mask a symptom, and if healing
does not occur spontaneously, then psychotherapy
is the greatest hope—plus drugs if necessary.
It is the old two-culture distrust and misunderstanding
that leads to narrow single-minded thinking.
Powerful drugs often have bad side effects.
The same goes for incorrectly used analysis and psychotherapy.
Given the psychology of despair and the availability
of drugs, dope, alcohol, cigarettes, food, and promiscuous sex,
it is a pipe dream to expect psychoactive drugs alone
to heal the human condition. Drugs numb the signal system,
and then we can't examine why the signals are on.

We need to work to create our psychic gyroscope
by which we become conscious of feedback
and respond to alter the psychological imbalance.
"Chemical imbalance" is both true and a tricky euphemism
that allows the easy denial of humanity
in homage to technology. There is also a psychic imbalance.

One might say that there is an alchemical imbalance.
Rather than cite Jungians on alchemy—because they are not
so understandable—I will quote one of Eric Hoffer's aphorisms:

In the alchemy of man's soul, almost all noble attributes—courage, honor, love, hope, faith, duty, loyalty—can be transmuted into ruthlessness. Compassion alone stands apart from the continuous traffic between good and evil proceeding within us. Compassion is the antitoxin of the soul: Where there is compassion even the most poisonous impulses remain relatively harmless. Thus the survival of the species may well depend on the ability to foster a boundless capacity for compassion. (Hoffer 1976, pp. 98–99)

We are all helmspersons in our life journeys.
We receive the signals from our conscious world
and from the sea of our unconscious.
Each of us steers as best we can. Although we travel
through fog, winds, storms, gales, the doldrums, and the unknown
(as well as delightful and pleasant weather),
although we struggle with the distortions
of our ego's "outsight," and our illusions and delusions, and
although we all, at some time or another, experience hallucinations
(if only hearing our name called when no one is there),
we are at the mercy not only of our environments
and other people, but especially of ourselves.
The *collective unconscious* gives us a unique handle
and vision into new ways of viewing our lives and our
struggles—the opportunity for *meaning.*

When we have exhausted our own self-help, to whom do we turn?
We turn to people we believe know or represent
what we seek. And when we find them, we discover
they don't know the answers, but they do know
how to help us discover that knowledge from within ourselves.
I think Machiavelli said, "Some people know everything,
and that's about all they know."

By accepting our fate, that is, *our present reality,*
we take the first step to change our destiny.
Our destination is another matter.
Dreams do not tell us what to do or where to go.

If one attributes such knowledge to the dream,
one abdicates responsibility.

RULES OF THUMB

Welcome your dreams no matter what they are.
Listen to them and write them down.
Honor and appreciate your innate creative power
that can conjure up such remarkable works of genius.
Sift your dreams. They are not all of equal importance.
Do not rely on simple interpretations—
that this always means that—because it doesn't.

Viewed with the proper attitude and appreciation, then
your dream will be your helper.
You can count on that.

Some Words About "Free Association"

Analysts Are Trained to Listen with a Third Ear Tuned to Associations

Just How Will an Analyst Listen to Your Associations?

Once in a while, in ordinary dialogue, we say, "What brought that to your mind?" when some comment seems to come from out of the blue or off the wall and there appears no obvious connection in the line of thought.

But there always is.

The analyst listens to the stream of your talking and tries to follow the associations you make for a clue to the puzzle being assembled. This is the disciplined art of psychotherapy.

Freud invented the technique known as "free association" in which the patient is asked to give his or her associations to an idea, feeling, dream phenomenon, fantasy, or whatever, and to let the mind roam freely wherever it goes, not to censor any thoughts. This line of associated thinking leads finally to the central conflict in the unconscious.

It depends also on what the central conflict is that the analyst constructs in his or her mind. Does it really make any difference whether you start free association from the dream or the street light? Jung felt it didn't make any difference because the mind always returned to the central conflict, provided you were not consciously censoring and editing what you said.

I do not think that *free association* is an important technique in contemporary psychoanalysis. In Jungian psychology, associations to dream fragments are essential, not freewheeling wherever it takes you, but directed *amplification.* The first thing that comes into your mind when you think about something is there for a reason. When a patient starts to tell me something, just in the telling, and hearing herself, and knowing I am listening, she may abruptly say:

"Oh, that reminds me of. . . ."

"For some strange reason, I recall now the time when. . . ."

"Oh, by the way, I just happened to think. . . ."

"I know this is far out, but it just occurred to me. . . ."

What follows *what* is important. The skill is in seeing the fit of connections and patterns—of bits. The art is in making simple comments that underscore the power of the patient's wisdom in comprehending the information.

Listening to Jungian analysts present cases—sometimes—I have an uncomfortable feeling that they are not as keen and sensitive to the flow of associations as those who have experienced it in a Freudian analysis.

But this is something that you can train yourself to notice, so to speak, to catch your thinking in mid-air, stop and see what comes to mind.

I will give you an example:

I dreamed that I opened a new, green, three-ring binder. All the pages inside were blank. For some reason the dream made me feel good. Suddenly, as I was shaving, I thought, *Of course! I felt good when I turned the pages over and the other sides were blank! I was* **turning over a new leaf!** That image confirmed the feeling of my well-being: I could trust it now. The image came from my own inner genie. The association of "new" to leaf is what did it.

When free association rambles, it is called "word salad." But word salad is not word garbage. Jung, who did the basic research on the Word Association Test, once commented on a delusional psychotic woman patient he had seen at the asylum in Zürich. She had been declared totally insane, and she would make remarks like "I am the Lorelei." To call herself the Lorelei meant to the doctors that she was mad. It made no sense. But did it? Jung remembered that just before she said that, she repeated a line from Heine's poem:

"Ich weiss nicht was soll es bedäuten."

(I do not know what it can possibly mean.)

Then she would say, "I am Socrates' deputy." Jung concluded that she was telling him and the people in the hospital that, like Socrates' deputy, she was falsely accused and that this label of insanity was wrongfully applied to her. Thus, no form of madness is so great that it does not have some sanity within it. She would say, "Naples and I between us supply the world with spaghetti." Jung thought that her phrases (or associations) made a kind of sense, that they represented a creative compensation in a profoundly troubled spirit; some sign of a feather still stirring with the life of a desire at heart to rise above this lack of recognition and unknowing experience in a despised, abnormal state; a longing to put oneself back once more in an important and useful role in the world of ordinary men and women. It was as if behind the dark, opaque screen of derangement, there stood another woman longing to join the life of her time, observing and deploring the tyranny of spirit standing between her and her desire (van der Post 1975, p. 113).

OK. I understand now. But how can we use that idea? We don't see many crazy people. How about giving me an example from your own experience?

I have a dialogue that I will read to you.

PATIENT: Next Tuesday is my fiftieth birthday. [The patient begins to sob like a child and she is silent for a long time.] I had no idea that I would be so emotional telling you that. [Pause. Composes herself.] I hope to have another fifty years.

    I listened without comment, asking myself, "Why indeed has she suddenly been overtaken with emotion and crying that makes me think of a little girl? With unexpected bursts of emotion, one wonders what has suddenly surfaced that makes her speechless." I thought, "Is it her fiftieth birthday? If so, why has she abruptly avoided talking about her sobbing and switched to her thought of wanting to live another fifty years? This is a place where it is safe to cry and show feelings—a place where confession is usually the order of the day—so why did she sweep her feelings under the rug?"

    As these thoughts ran through my mind, she sat in silent repose and after a while began to talk softly.

PATIENT: My closest friend's mother died and I wanted to be at her funeral. I knew it would mean a lot to my friend. [She spoke more about the funeral which she didn't attend.]

WILMER: [Age fifty . . . sobbing like a child . . . death of a mother . . . a funeral. She hopes to live on and on for another fifty. She sees herself at the middle of her life. She wanted to comfort someone else's grief, like a sister perhaps . . . What did this have to do with her life at this particular moment? And also here with me? I say nothing. My eyes do not leave her.]

PATIENT: I felt the same way when I gave another friend a special gift that I had made. It wasn't expensive, but I had spent a lot of my time making it. He [sic] didn't even show emotion. I wanted a genuine response which meant he understood.

WILMER: [She means me. She wants a genuine understanding *response* from me—someone I represent. It seems to me that her use of the word *genuine* sounds unusual, and therefore significant. For someone not to respond is one thing but feigned or inauthentic responsiveness is worse. Her gift was caring. She felt guilty for not caring enough for her friend. Had some grief of her own taken over? I keep on with this inner dialogue, attentive. She seems quite satisfied that I am just there, really there.]

PATIENT: I guess I'm just rambling.

WILMER: [No. It is all connected, but now she is asking me if it makes sense to me. If she brings me a gift, will I respond? Yes, I will.] I don't think you are rambling, but you seem to have gone away from the sadness that came over you when you mentioned your fiftieth birthday. Yet it all seems connected. Do you think so?

PATIENT: I think I was wanting someone to care for me. I wanted to feel that I deserved that care, that love. Not to feel guilty or undeserving. I had to feel that it was genuine. I wonder what the derivation of that word is?

WILMER: Let's look it up. [No hesitation about should I do this or should I not do this? No games, like "Let's talk about why you want to know the derivation." I know why. I sense it is a significant word to her. It turns out that we both want to know about the derivation of *genuine.* No "Why do you ask?" Just "Let's look it up." I get out the dictionary.]

genuine *(d e'njuin* †*natural, Native; not spurious or counterfeit. L. genuinus, f. genu KNEE; the orig. ref. was to the recognition of a new-born child by a father placing it on his knees; later assoc. with genus race, KIN . . . (Oxford Dictionary of English Etymology, p. 394)*

PATIENT: That clicked! [She talks about her associations: memories of death, loss, rejection, hypocrisy, and her search for her father. She feels he has never been there for her in her life crises.]

WILMER: Talk to me about your search for your father, and the father's search to recognize a newborn child by placing it on his knees.

PATIENT: [She responds, and then, as the hour draws to an end, she says:] Oh. I remember something I want to tell you that comes to mind. I went to church Sunday. There was a lot of kneeling. I felt like I was facing my God in my prayers . . . even though I was not genuflecting like the rest of the congregation. I had the feeling that it was all right with the priest because when I looked up, I saw his benign acceptance.

WILMER: You were standing up for what you believed.

PATIENT: Yes. I guess the theme of today is to be genuine.

WILMER: Yes, the theme of today *is* genuine. [After saying goodbye, she left, obviously deep in feeling thought.]

[The patient later gave me permission to use this material.]

Wouldn't it have been easy to talk to the patient specifically, saying that she felt that I was genuine and benignly accepting her like her priest? Wouldn't it have been simple to end the hour talking about the transference and me? Yes, but that would have been narcissistic intrusion. She had come. She had brought her labor and her gift. She had searched for the father who was both priest and me, as well as her real father and her symbolic father. The theme of *being genuine* is not only simpler, however, but it also allowed her to leave with her feet on the ground rather than a head full of psychology. After sobbing like a child, she walked out of the session having found meaning in her tears, and her silence.

My associations—for myself, not for her—as she left, involved the salt of tears: "You are the salt of the earth; but if salt has lost its taste, how shall its saltiness be restored?" (Matt. 5:13–16).

The World Within and the World Without

It is common parlance for Jungians to speak
of the *inner world* and the *outer world,*
referring to the psyche and to external reality.
We all know about the outer world we are born into,
live and die in. But what about before and after?
Being born is a world-shattering experience.
Once the umbilical cord is cut
and the first gasp and cry come,
there is no way back.

In our psyches, we have never totally left that womb.
We know this by fantasies of paradise,
the Garden of Eden and the Fall,
bliss and perfection unattainable
in the ordinary world.
The womb is the essence and vision of security
and oneness with the eternal mother.

The experience of birth
is the realization of creation,
and its end in death
evokes the image of rebirth,
rejuvenation, and immortality.
Even before birth, before conception,
there was world and being,
which made possible our own creation.
We can hypothesize from clinical experience
and genetic theory that the psyche,
like the body, follows an inherited,
evolutionary thread from prehistoric times.

In the outer world, our physical and spiritual beings
interact with our total environment.
Jung postulated a collective unconscious,
which bears no actual connection
with the world of our personal life
in the world we call physical.

The *collective unconscious,* being historic
and prehistoric, antedates our conception.
We are born, so to speak, with our psychic imprint

from time immemorial.
From this inner world, we will learn
as much as (or more than) from the outer world.
We experience the collective unconscious
most clearly in our dreams and our symbolic life.
Jung called the collective unconscious the *objective unconscious*
because it was not subjective or personal
like the *personal unconscious,*
which Freud had discovered from dreams and—

**Stop! This is getting to be a discourse in general psychology. How about a
rundown on the site between the conscious outer and the unconscious inner
world?**

Okay. At the border between the inner world and the outer world,
is our *persona:* Its face is to the outside,
its back side hidden or disguised by the mask on the outside.
Persona is the symbol of the *archetype* that Jung named for the
mask worn by the Greek actors: the public expression of face
of the part being played.

With a persona, we present ourselves
and our social and external roles.
The persona is revealed by our faces, our clothes,
our body movements, and all the trappings
that we use to tell the outer world who we are.

With our personas, we often attempt to present our idealized
selves, our *ego-ideals.*
Therefore, it hides our shadows and protects us
from the shadows of others.
It is a kind of acceptable sham.
Take the persona of the analyst:
clothing, facial expression, body movement, gestures,
demeanor, movement, and voice, as well as the office, car, etc.,
proclaim the persona.
If the analyst identifies with his or her persona—
that is, believes it is the true inner self—
there is big trouble.

What do you mean, *big trouble* by identifying with your persona?

The analyst becomes the stereotype
and is inflated with the impression that he or she has no shadow.
This can be prevented:
when we are learning a role and playing our persona,
we can facilitate its authenticity
by learning to play in the sense that a child naturally creates.
It is learning to playact in order to act the play.

Who can teach us this?

People in the helping professions
who have years of experience,
diligence, intelligence and aplomb. . . .

And aplomb!

Especially *aplomb,*
or poise, and equanimity. . . .

And equanimity!

Especially equanimity,
from the Latin *aequus,*
"equal" plus *animus,* "mind" or "soul,"
meaning "to bear with equal mind." Thus equanimity
embodies composure and emotional balance,
especially under stress.
It is the epitome of inner and outer world symmetry and harmony.

Oh. OK.

PART

THREE

I PREFER TO LOOK PEOPLE IN THE EYE.
I KNOW SOME THERAPISTS PUT PATIENTS
ON THE COUCH. BUT THERE IS A LOT
YOU NEVER SEE IF YOU NEVER SEE THE
PATIENT'S SEEING YOU.

The Personality of the Therapist Counts

How in the world could anyone know what kind of therapist to see? Jungian? Freudian? Gestalt? Transactional? Holistic? Counselor? Yellow page lottery? Ask your doctor? Clergy? Friend? Or flip a coin?

It takes courage and wisdom to seek help when you need it. It is a matter of strength, not a sign of weakness. But, as you ask, *how do you find the right therapist?*

In all candor, you need a little bit of luck—sans impulse. But there is a *basic principle:*

> Be sure you have a positive, trusting feeling
> for the competence and integrity of the therapist.
> Do not, repeat, *do not* work with someone you
> do not like. Don't waste precious time and money
> in "working through" basic trust.

RULE OF THUMB

When the patient comes into the office,
do not say, "Have a nice day."
Say, "How are you?"
He will answer, "I'm fine."
Then you get down to business. . . .

"I AM NOT ANGRY!"

"I AM NOT ANGRY!"

"I AM NOT ANGRY!"

"I AM NOT ANGRY!"

What is the therapist like? You can't just tell by appearances, but a great deal is revealed in appearance and your intuitive judgment. They come in all types and all sorts of training and experience. Be careful who you choose and whether or not you continue with that person. It is a tryout for both of you in the beginning.

Most people who are depressed do not like themselves.
You don't need two don't-likes.
You gotta like one of them to begin with.
If someone you know has been treated by a therapist,
shows the worth of the therapy, and will give a recommendation—
be thankful.
Although professional societies will give you recommendations,
even that is chancy.

It used to be said that the method was the essential thing.
Jung always maintained that the *personality*
    of the therapist
    was the most important factor in psychological treatment.

Credentials count, of course,
with a probability of quality in proportion to them,
    but diplomas and certificates are only pieces of paper.
I know some people with great credentials
who would be better off changing light bulbs.

It sounds to me like gambling in a casino, like pulling a card out of a deck.

Not really. That's telephone directory roulette.
Still, when one is desperate, one takes chances.
Remember, you may be embarking on a long journey,
where you will reveal your most intimate life
and your soul.

A warning:
There is always a risk of landing in the lap of
a seductive therapist.
Love in the transference occurs naturally,
and there is no anesthesia for it.
But sex in therapy is incest.
There is an *absolute rule of thumb:*
No sex.

Transference is one of the most powerful forces known.
You have every reason to expect your therapist
to understand countertransference.
A second warning:
    Don't take it for granted. See if it is so.
What are the basic expectations of a therapist and therapy?
    Skill at the task of therapy—
    Enough intelligence to comprehend—
    Compassion is the heart of the business—
    Mutual trust in a professional relationship.

What do I do with those lofty ideas?

Do your best.
That's all any of us can do.

Let's get down to the facts. What could I expect if I were in psychotherapy?

Well, I can't tell you what would happen because
therapists, analysts, psychiatrists, and psychologists are
all different individually. Personality, experience,
and training create different people.

What's more, there are so many different methods and schools
of psychological help, it would be impossible to answer
generally.

Now that's a cop-out. You are a Jungian analyst, so what would I expect if I saw a Jungian therapist?

Like I just said, I can't tell you what would happen because
analysts are all different—individually, and
personality-wise . . . like I said.
And different Jungians use different approaches,
although they follow some common principles resembling the topic of
this book. It would be. . . .

I know . . . "impossible to answer generally." Well, give me an answer that isn't general.

OK. I assume you are going to see a certified Jungian analyst, not someone who simply calls himself or herself "Jungian" or "Jungian trained." That's the first determination since there's a lot of brush in the woodpile.

People who are not deeply read or experienced or trained, who are superficially acquainted with Jung, have a tendency to take some strange tacks. Some are even weird. Others are not. As a matter of fact, some Jungian analysts who are indeed certified aren't . . . well, they aren't up to snuff.

"Aren't up to snuff!" That makes me gag. Talk turkey.

You are right. I was being diplomatic because I didn't want to say anything negative about some of my colleagues. But some of them have hang-ups that have never been analyzed. You see, what makes analysts different from other therapists is that they must experience personal analysis to qualify as psychoanalysts. Don't you see? It's like talking about "doctors." I must admit some are not good analysts. You have to see for yourself; listen to people who have been in analysis with a specific analyst to see how those patients view that analyst. Then you must *make up your own mind* after an interview or two. My advice is to follow your hunches; trust your instincts. If the analyst seems right for you, give it a try. If you are doubtful or skeptical or even negative, then forget that person. If you are in therapy with him or her and find it intolerable, stop. Find the right person, at least someone you feel and think is right for you.

Oh, for God's sake. How can I shop for a Jungian analyst when there are barely two thousand in the world? I'd be lucky to find one or two in a big city.

I know it is tough. But suppose you do find an analyst whom you like and trust. *If you stick to the analysis, really commit your energies and your Self to working, listening, and being prepared to learn,* then over time you will learn. You have to have stick-to-itiveness.

Stick-to-itiveness?

No. I mean you must stick to it! The Jungian approach is no feather bed. You can expect to struggle, to like, to dislike, to love, and hate your analyst at different times. Some patients are really fortunate in that they like their analysts from beginning to end, don't deify them, and don't expect more than a well-trained professional person with feet of clay as well as some unusual gifts and knowledge, and who is more interested in the patient than in themselves.

Jungian analysis demands that you take a hard look at your psyche and dreams, and also at the world in which you live and work. It requires an appreciation of the symbolic world and an ability to tolerate ambiguity and strange dreams.

Let me give you an example. A patient made her first appointment to see me. The night before she came to my office, she dreamed:

> *There is a knock at my door. I open it. No one is there, but a letter has been left at my feet. The envelope has my name on it, but no address and no stamp. The letter says, "Please come and see me. Something has happened and it is a vial experience." It was spelled v-i-a-l so I looked up* vial *in the dictionary and it said a vial is a sealed container. I looked in one of my Jung books and read about containers and alchemical retorts and symbols of transformation. I thought that the experience I was going to have seeing you would be such a container and transforming experience.*

I asked her if it was possible that the sender of the message had misspelled *vial.* Did she think that either way it might mean something different from what she had found?

"What do you think it means to have a 'vial experience'?" I asked her.

Then she told me why she came to see me. She thought that she couldn't say what kind of experience that might be. She wondered who had delivered the letter, and who the sender was. It could have been vial, vile, or vital, or . . . "but I guess what it means is that I was trying to find the answer in Jung. What do you think?"

"I think that's a good start."

I'm beginning to see what it might be like. But I think I will just read your book and do my homework and be my own helper for now.

You get it! I'm not selling Jungian analysis, but I am trying to give Jung a hearing. He hasn't always had that chance. I'll try to explain in a way Einstein once recommended: be as simple as possible and no simpler.

Face-to-Face Therapy

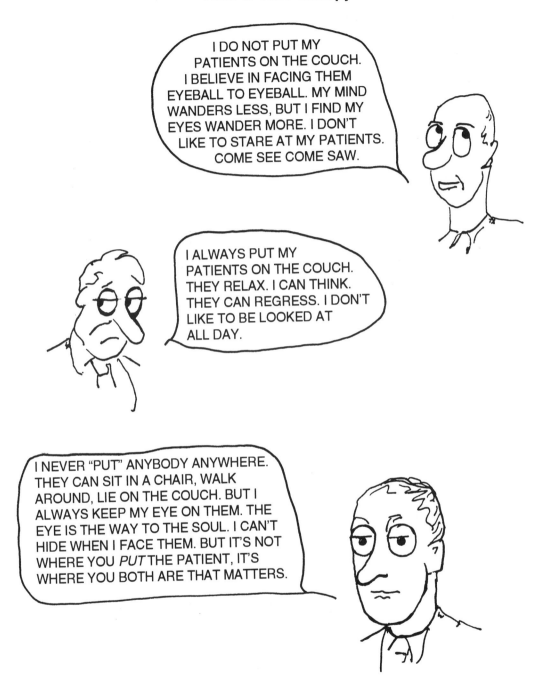

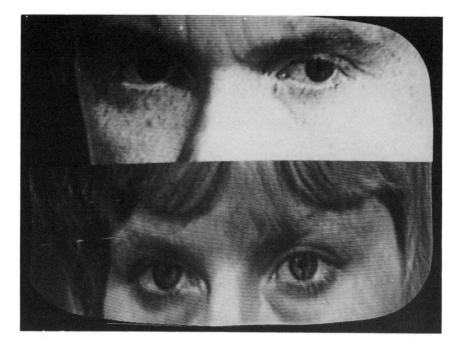

A doctor and a patient sit facing each other. A TV camera takes a picture of one from over the shoulder of the other and by a special effect the monitor will show only the eyes of each looking at the other. If you will follow the session watching their eyes, you hardly have to know what they are saying in order to see how they are attentive or avoiding, and how alert the doctor is to the subtle nuances of the patient. You can tell a lot about what is happening.

Photograph of television monitor from supervision of a psychiatrist and patient in therapy (Wilmer 1968, pp. 129–133).

When you look into the eyes of a patient and the patient looks into your eyes, you both see one another much deeper than the pupil. For a moment you might even see the heart and soul. But suppose you wanted the patient to see herself—it could be done—and even talk to herself. You may do this by videotaping her with two cameras from different angles, and superimposing the objects. The technology gives you an amazing human experience. . . .

Photograph from black-and-white television monitor.

The television monitor shows the two images of the patient as she talks with me. By superimposing the images so that the foreground figure is dark and the background figure is shaded gray and ghostlike, one has the impression of the patient observing herself while she looks at the doctor. When she first saw this picture, she exclaimed, as if it was an important discovery, "I'm not ugly!" She was asked to talk with the image in the picture (which one was her choice) as she listened to the sound track and saw the videotape replaying the interview. She asked me to do the same, as there were two cameras on me also. In this way, it was possible to reconstruct an inner dialogue which was unspoken as the interview proceeded.

Rule of Thumb Rule

A Dialogue Between Two Jungian Analysts

She said,   "I don't believe in rules."

He said,   "You ought to."

She said,   "That's just the point! I don't want anybody telling me what I *ought* to do and what I *ought not* to do."

He said,   "Why not?"

She said,   "Because rules are made to be broken."

He said,   "Like the Golden Rule?"

She said,   "I don't believe in the Golden Rule, but I expect you to treat me as I would treat myself: make no rules."

He said,   "You are a Jungian analyst who had to adhere to certain rules to get where you got."

She said,   "The more rules there are, the more rule-breakers there are. The more laws that are written, the more criminals there are. Those in power who know what they want can make rules for others to obey."

He said,   "You expect your patients to show up for their appointments on time, right?"

She said,   "Right, and if they do not, then we analyze it. Not a broken rule, but a psychological phenomenon.
Each person should learn right from wrong.
Jung said that people should 'follow their own law.'"

He said,   "Yes, their *inner* law. He didn't say there should be no outer law rules. How could we judge what we think is right or wrong if we didn't have rules or laws to weigh our opinions against?"

She said,   "For a reasonably bright person, you are really quite thick-headed. The point is to be *nonjudgmental:* Do not judge."

He said,   "That sounds like a rule to me: Thou shalt not judge. Don't you think that there is really a need for ethical rules to protect patients or clients from sexual exploitation?"

She said,   "Who's to say what is sexual exploitation? There is always sexuality. I don't think there should be rules against sex."

He said,   "You know that sexual relations between patients and therapists constitutes malpractice."

She said,   "You can't make rules about sex."

RULE OF THUMB RULE: You Can.

Psychotherapy as the Spiral of the Nautilus

Let us consider therapy or analysis as an ever-widening, ever-expanding spiral.

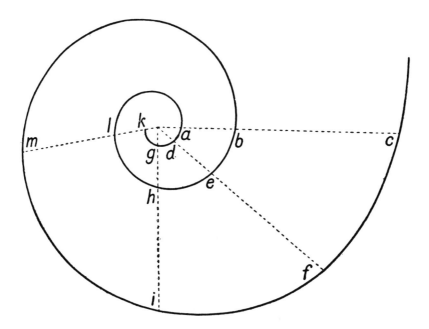

Spiral of the Nautilus
Diagram from Thompson (1942, p. 771)

The equiangular spiral of the shell of the nautilus constantly expands so that the inner spiral is always exactly one-third of the outer spiral. For example, *ab* is one-third of *bc*, and so on with the other radii. The numerical ratio is one of unusual simplicity. In *Practical Jung*, I used the Archimedes spiral as the visual image of psychotherapy, but that spiral's whorls wrap around each other like a sailor would wind a rope on the deck of a ship. The present image is not of a solid movement, but of a container that opens to the sea. You might call it a way of visualizing individuation. This is a mechanical image, and one must remember that it is merely the diagram of a growing organism.

Year after year beheld the silent toil
That spread his lustrous coil;
Still, as the spiral grew,
He left the past year's dwelling for the new,
Stole with soft step its shining archway through,
Built up its idle door,
Stretched in his last-found home, and knew the old no more.

Build thee more stately mansions, O my soul,
As the swift seasons roll!
Leave thy low-vaulted past!
Let each new temple, nobler than the last,
Shut thee from heaven with a dome more vast,
Till thou at length are free,
Leaving thine outgrown shell by life's unresting sea!

Oliver Wendell Holmes, "The Chambered Nautilus"

Flow Image for the Process of a Therapy Hour

Imagine the therapist and the patient sitting and talking to each other. The time from start to finish will be designated as one hour. First imagine the flow on a flat piece of graph paper that one can diagrammatically follow from left to right. This straight, linear flow would not rise above or below the paper nor have a front and back. Such an image is a biopsy of time, for the beginning and end are simply sliced off arbitrarily, leaving the impression that the whole process in this form began before and continued after the one-hour time boundary.

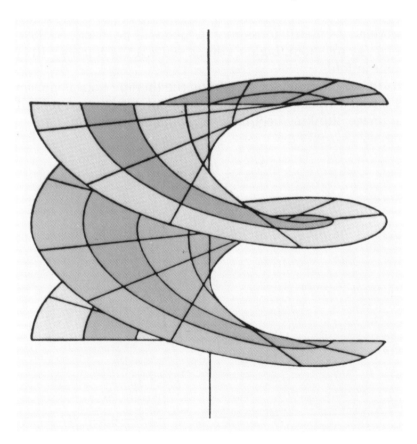

Right circular helix as an image of the flow of the process in a therapy session.*

---

*The right helicoid is a circular helix on the surface of which are drawn asyntonic lines forming an orthogonal net of minimal surfaces. The polar line is a central reference point (Stuik 1961, p. 20).

Now imagine the circular helix and looking down on a diagram from the top as it unfolds from below to above. It will look like a changing polar diagram revolving around the central pole. The surfaces, which are known minimal surfaces, represent the containing area for both sides of the dialogue/interaction. The central pathway on both sides of the surface represents the ordered logical flow of interaction. On the areas to either side are the associations, fantasies, feelings, and all aspects and behavior that are not articulated.

One may divide the flow into quartiles or any segment and identify the patterns. Also one may take out any boundary area as an entity itself or in the context of the entire helix. Imagine this right circular helix as a predetermined geometric form upon which will be inscribed the code patterns of any one hour. Lights, colors, signs, and symbols will appear as the hour unfolds.

This image or model for imagining the therapy hour is presented to give the reader a visual gestalt, and a different perspective. It is a four-function image: thinking, feeling, intuition, and sensation.

Inner Dialogue/Inner Speech

They Are Related But Separate Functions of the Brain

*Pure word-dumbness (subcortical motor aphasia). Uttered speech is disturbed as in expressive aphasia, **but inner speech** is intact, comprehension is unimpaired, and writing is normal. The lesion is thought to lie in the white matter in Broca's area.*

(Hinsie and Campbell 1973, p. 56)

The inner dialogue in the therapist's mind provides the incredible creative preparation for speaking. At the same time, however, an inner dialogue occurs in the patient's mind. It is as if the conversation occurs on two levels. Many playwrights, novelists, artists, and poets have made this a brilliant literary device. In Wagner's *Ring of the Nibelungen,* for example, Siegfried, faced with the monster, lets us know his inner dialogue. This talk is not just preconscious, or a construct of psychology; it occurs not merely in the mind, but also in the physical brain in a specific manner. Many great discoveries of neurology, neuroanatomy, and neuroscience have been made in patients with brain lesions from trauma, disease, or developmental defects.

It is significant that in cases of subcortical motor aphasia (when there is a lesion in the white matter of a small area of the left lower frontal brain cortex) inner speech is intact and comprehension as well as writing are normal, but expressive speech or outer dialogue is impaired or blocked. This establishes an autonomy of inner dialogue suggesting a more primitive nature to inner speech in human comprehension. It might be that we talked to ourselves before we learned to talk to others. So we ridicule people for talking to themselves as if this in itself is crazy while it may be our elemental sanity. The significance to linguistics or language is beyond my discussion here. Yet disciplined self-training in conscious inner dialogue as a rehearsal for outer dialogue might be a biological clue to empathy and thinking.

What do you mean: "When you are talking to me, I am talking to myself"!? Sounds crazy.

Inner dialogue with myself or with you, unspoken, is normal. This is the way I can think before I talk.

So! That's what you are doing when you won't talk to me. Like I was saying to myself . . . yesterday . . .

FOUR

This typology stuff is really quite simple to understand and use. The trouble you are having is due to your type.

Typology: Extraversion/Introversion

Each one of us is predominately extraverted or introverted.
To be infatuated with your individual uniqueness
is to be one-sided.
To be wed to statistical norms, averages, and science
is to be one-sided.

The odd one, the misfit, the rare bird,
the maverick, the exceptional one, and the nonconformist
may range from genius to irritant, from saint to madman.

Go back to this typology business you were talking about. What type am I?

You're an extraverted, outgoing busybody.
I don't particularly like high-powered extraverts like you.
They are too showy, too talky, too everything.
But that's because I'm an introvert.
I like to be by myself, and I don't have a lot of friends.
I am fascinated by dreams and imagination.

Is it either one way or the other? Is the world made up of either/or? Aren't we all a bit of both?

Of course! Being outgoing or turning inward
are two sides of our attitude.
The question is, where are you on that continuum?
How far are you from the balanced midpoint between
a healthy extraversion and a healthy introversion,
or an extreme of either?

According to Jungian typology,
our conscious attitude is either extraverted or introverted.
Our unconscious is the opposite.

That's heavy-duty stuff. So I'm an extravert and my unconscious is introverted? What the devil does that mean?

It means that when you are bedeviled,
it is your introverted side that gets to you.
You see, extraverts generally
are intolerant of introverts and vice versa.
Intolerance arises because the opposite types
represent the inferior, undeveloped side.
That's the Jungian way of seeing prejudice.
We tend to fear and distrust what is strange and different.
It is fantastic that people generally fall in love

with individuals of the opposite type,
with someone who represents what is incomplete in themselves,
with what, when united with them, would make them whole.
On the other hand, we tend to have friends of the same type.

**I guess American culture is extraverted. We like our children to be outgoing
and when they are not, we think something is wrong with them. The real
American is a back-slapping, smiling, friendly person in tune with "Hail, hail,
the gang's all here."**

Right. That is the American stereotype and cultural norm.
That personality type devalues introspection, reflective attitudes.
A less aggressive, less "must-win" life
is depreciated as inferior. It is not inferior.
Because the odd one, the different one, the strange one
who doesn't conform to the norm may have the very
talents, gifts, and creative imagination that our culture needs.

Jung recognized that these two different type *attitudes*
determine how each individual perceives the world and people.
Each will see the same things in opposite ways.

Nothing is odd about *either* extraversion *or* introversion.
It is the extremes that are abnormal.
The excessively introverted person is called *schizoid*.
The most extreme introverts are schizophrenic.
The excessively extroverted person is called hypomanic.
The most extreme extrovert is manic.
The introverted person may suffer painful isolation in America,
but be quite comfortable in introverted Switzerland.
A schizoid Eskimo would fit the Arctic culture.
A schizoid flamenco dancer, however, would be freakish.

An extravert would make a good used-car salesperson,
but a disturbed extraverted person would be hysterical.
The hypomanic person, when under control, is apt to be a whiz
at whatever he or she is doing. The extreme manic is not,
being too much, going to too many places, taking too many
                 actions, spending too much money.
and speeding toward overcommitment and loss of control
with flights of ideas and energy consumed in disjointed actions.

The extreme extravert may fall from a high
into almost total inaction and depression.
When the depression and mania alternate
it is called bi-polar disorder or manic depression.

You're always thinking about your self! When you get enthusiastic you close your mouth. You react so damn slowly and nobody seems to really know you. Why do you hide from the public? That's where the world is. That's where the action is! Assert yourself! You're always sort of closing doors.

Why am I supposed to be like you? You get enthusiastic at the drop of a hat and you start gabbing and yacking. You are always talking on the phone and going places. Why don't you stop and reflect? You may be personality girl but why don't you slow down? Everything comes off the top of your head.

EXTRAVERT TYPE   INTROVERT TYPE

Jung observed that we are born with a dominant type,
which is probably a genetic trait.
It is not fixed, though, and varies throughout our lifetimes.
During the first half of life, being an extravert is an asset.
Energy and activities directed toward accomplishment,
achievement, building career, work, home, and family
demand outer orientation and action.
On the other hand, the introvert has it better
in the second half of life, with the need to adapt
to the diminishing of life and toward inner growth and wisdom.
As the child comes into the world of expanding horizons,
the older person is in the afternoon and evening of life
and the fulfillment of life in death.
To strive to be eternally young is failure to grow.

So, what am I, an extravert, to learn from you, a navel-gazing introvert? It sounds like this typology stuff is a sophisticated cop-out.

What *you* can learn from me
is exactly what *I* can learn from you,
that people of opposite types see the same things oppositely.
Both points of view are valid.

Each person has his or her own subjective truth.
I remember a very introverted man
who was bitterly unhappy and angry
with his remarkably extraverted wife
whom I was seeing in analysis.
He wanted to talk with me
because I was hearing everything only from his wife's
point of view.
His wife and I agreed that it was a good idea.
Of course, she felt she was absolutely right and he was wrong.

I listened to him as he poured out his story.
Then abruptly he became silent
and to his astonishment, began to cry.
He had expected in me a critic like his wife,
who would explain his wife.
Instead, all I wanted was to listen.
When he stopped crying, I said,
"I want to hear your truth."
My words astonished him, and he told me.
Then he said, "I guess my wife's truth is different.
I never thought of it that way."

That helps me to understand. It's like conflict between individuals, collectives, within minorities, and between minorities and majorities. It is a gender and an ethnic struggle for understanding, the way enemies see each other. Yet I would hate to think of watered-down truths, and the idea that everything was wishy-washy relative. There *are* fundamental truths.

The great truths of one era of science
often turn out to be false in another time.
What seems vague and uncertain
may turn out to be vague and uncertain.
To tolerate uncertainty and even ambiguity
may mark the ability to cope with the life process itself.
One must hold one's truths, one's facts, one's convictions,
although these are not sacred.
What is sacred is another realm.
It was Jung's wisdom and his struggle
that allowed for the spiritual, the sacred,
the religious, and the mysteries of life
to be an essential part of analytical psychology.

The Four Functions of Typology:
Thinking/Feeling/Intuition/Sensation

After the two attitude types of **introversion** and **extraversion,**
Jung described four **function types.**
There are two pairs of opposites
on the same kind of continuum as introversion/extraversion.

Thinking——Feeling

Intuition——Sensation

These typologies may be used to describe the conscious personality.

You have one **dominant** function type, and therefore you face the world
as a
    Thinking type,
      a *Feeling* type,
        an *Intuitive* type,
          or a *Sensation* type.
One is your strongest, most developed function.
In addition to the dominant function,
a second function is next in prominence.
It is called the *auxiliary* function.

**It's getting complicated. I'll try to put it together and figure out my type. I
would say that I'm an extraverted, thinking type with an auxiliary sensation
function. That makes us good sparring partners since you are the opposite, I
think.**

Correct.
And when you figure yourself out, you know a lot
about how other types perceive and evaluate the world
and see different truths through different windows.

Let us take two functions.
Since *thinking* and *feeling* are opposite ways of judging,
you cannot do them both at the same time.
That is a basic fact.
For example, the thinking scientist must not look
at experimental data and say "I feel that these are correct."
Colleagues would laugh the scientist off the block.
Feelings are not acceptable in pure science,
although they *are* powerfully present,

Vermont Senator Patrick J. Leahy's neighbors are determinedly protective of his privacy. A traveler on the dirt road near the Leahy farmhouse asked of a neighbor, "Senator Leahy live up this way?"

Neighbor: "Are you a relative?"
Traveler: "No."
Neighbor: "A friend of his?"
Traveler: "No."
Neighbor: "He expecting you?"
Traveler: "No."
Neighbor: "Never heard of him."*

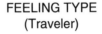

SENSATION TYPE
(Neighbor)

FEELING TYPE
(Traveler)

but they are put aside *as if* they were not there.
Thinking is conscious and feeling is unconscious.
Thus, the *thinker* strives for consciousness and rationality,
dismissing the irrational unconscious.
The analyst who deals also with the illogical
must often see beyond the rational logic of linear thinking.
Conclusions are then drawn from intuition and feeling.
Feeling judgment is just as valid as thinking judgment,
but not in the same context or places.

Feeling function refers not to *emotional* feelings,
but to feeling that something is right or wrong, good or bad.
Feeling types are more naturally adaptive to relationships—
the extroverts to many, introverts to a few.
Thinking people who live in their heads,
especially if they are introverted,
are awkward and poor at relationships.

Just for the record,
Jung called the dominant function
the *superior function,* and
and its opposite the *inferior function.*
He did not mean one was better than the other,
only that one was above in the consciousness
and the other below in the unconscious.

*Copyright © 1986 by The New York Times Company. Reprinted by permission.

**I would prefer an airplane pilot to be a thinking person and not feel the way to
land in the fog, but I would prefer the flight attendant to be a feeling type.**

INTUITIVE TYPE   SENSATION TYPE

The other pair of opposite functions consist of
intuition and *sensation.*
The intuitive person perceives the world
as if seeing around corners
almost by mysterious extrasensory perception.
Sometimes we say that such people are *sensitive,*
as if they have invisible antennae.

Discoveries are often made by intuitive hunches
and a bit of luck that contradict theory and logic.
Louis Pasteur said,
"In the field of observation,
chance favors only the prepared mind" (Auden and Kronenberger
1962, p. 347).

Sudden revelations and inspiration are intuitive,
sometimes even divine.
Having intuition is like being gifted.
You don't have to work hard at it.
Intuition seems to send its messages out of the blue.
Yet, it is only as good as disciplined experience makes it.
One can have some pretty kooky intuitions.
One can lose all one's money on a bad investment hunch.

I know some therapists who think (*sic*) they are *intuitive*
when they reach their conclusions through *feelings.*
They believe being *intuitive*
is the distinctive trait of a good therapist.

I am a feeling type.
One day I was driving on the highway with my eight-year-old son.
We passed an accident where the police, rescue squad,
and ambulance were on the scene. Trying to diminish
his fear, I said, "Isn't it great
that the rescue squads are there?
Aren't they doing a wonderful job?" My child,
a realist and sensation-minded child, replied,
"I dunno. It isn't over yet."

Intuitive people tend to fly from thing to thing,
avoiding the hard work of getting the facts, and they
often sow and do not reap.
Jungian analysts, Freudian analysts, and depth psychologists
risk the seductive power of their own formulations
and the dazzle of their field, thereby becoming inflated.
A built-in, potential remedy occurs
when our four functions are in balance,
when they compensate for each other,
and we are in touch with the Self
and therefore centered.
It is not altogether "the times" that make for the heightened
awareness and prevalence of *narcissism:*

It Id us!

Sensation does not mean sensational.
A highly developed banker or accountant will be
sensation-minded and unsensational.
A thinking-minded professor of mathematics
with good sensation may not know how to make friends
or put together a recipe for goulash or blueberry muffins.

Thinkers distrust Feelers who demean Thinkers.
Intuitives have scant regard for Sensation people
who think Intuitives are kind of crazy.
Once again, it is worthwhile thinking about these type
differences in understanding *prejudice.*

Jung said that identification with one particular function
at once produces a tension of opposites.
The more compulsive the one-sidedness, and the more untamed
the libido which streams off to one side,
the more daemonic it becomes.
Involuntary one-sidedness
is a sign of barbarism (Jung 1921, par. 346–347).

Oh, to be a Thinker
in the land of Feelers!
Or a Feeler in the Thinker world.
But I would rather be a Sensation
on the island of Intuition
than an extravert examining his navel
in an introverted lotus position.

That sounds as if you are not satisfied where you are.

And what do you intuit from that?

**I think you are trying to give me a message, like
time to go on to the next topic.**

Yes.

She: Thinking/Sensation
He: Feeling/Intuitive

She: Intuitive/Feeling
He: Sensation/Thinking

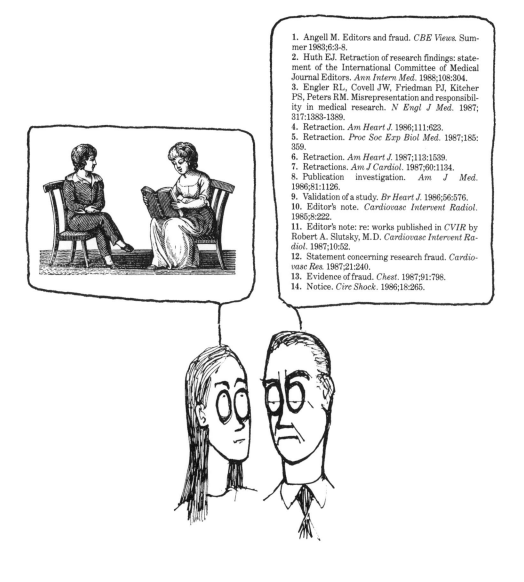

1. Angell M. Editors and fraud. *CBE Views.* Summer 1983;6:3-8.
2. Huth EJ. Retraction of research findings: statement of the International Committee of Medical Journal Editors. *Ann Intern Med.* 1988;108:304.
3. Engler RL, Covell JW, Friedman PJ, Kitcher PS, Peters RM. Misrepresentation and responsibility in medical research. *N Engl J Med.* 1987; 317:1383-1389.
4. Retraction. *Am Heart J.* 1986;111:623.
5. Retraction. *Proc Soc Exp Biol Med.* 1987;185: 359.
6. Retraction. *Am Heart J.* 1987;113:1539.
7. Retractions. *Am J Cardiol.* 1987;60:1134.
8. Publication investigation. *Am J Med.* 1986;81:1126.
9. Validation of a study. *Br Heart J.* 1986;56:576.
10. Editor's note. *Cardiovasc Intervent Radiol.* 1985;8:222.
11. Editor's note: re: works published in *CVIR* by Robert A. Slutsky, M.D. *Cardiovasc Intervent Radiol.* 1987;10:52.
12. Statement concerning research fraud. *Cardiovasc Res.* 1987;21:240.
13. Evidence of fraud. *Chest.* 1987;91:798.
14. Notice. *Circ Shock.* 1986;18:265.

PART

FIVE

The Unconscious Can Be Your Enemy: You Are the Enemy

The "If-Onlies"

> . . . man, however great his knowledge, will never know the riches or the broad intellectual domains that are illuminated by the conscious act of *constructing.* And it was from the human mind that even the gods received their gift of *creation,* because that mind, being periodic and abstract, can expand any of its conceptions to the point where they are no longer conceivable.
>
> (Valery 1894, p. 71)

A common problem people have is that they live in the past with bitter regrets or fantasied delights. When one is tormented by "if-onlies," "could-have-beens," "might-have-beens," and "should-have-beens," one does not live in the present. Other people who seem unable to stay rooted firmly in the here and now live in the future by "what-ifs" and "I-coulds" and the fantasies of elusive but seductive "go-for-its," "get-the-hell-outa-heres," and "tomorrow-and-tomorrows." The cure for being pulled to the past or pushed to the future is to stay put.

Staying put is not forever. It is for now—not "just for now" but for the now that is our eternity. Yesterdays are gone and tomorrows never come. To live to be remembered by the future is the disastrous fate of Ozymandias, a once mighty king in Percy Shelley's poem, "Ozymandias," whose image crumbled in the desert of time. The power that possesses a person and overcomes better judgment is the force of the unconscious. It is as if one is possessed by an archetype. We are literally unable to free ourselves until we face the archetype, and to do that we cannot run away. The archetype will always follow us, and if we outrun it, it will be there waiting to greet us when we arrive. But when we face it, it backs down.

In ages past, people spoke of being haunted by the ghosts of the dead or memories of the past. You have all known people who close the window shades on today and sink into the morass of yesterday. You all know people who fly on clouds into the wild blue yonder, always going somewhere great, but they never arrive.

The cure, as I said, is to live to the lees in the present. In ordinary common sense parlance, live day by day, each day being sufficient unto itself. Warning signs and psychological hooks catch us. They are:

> *if only.* . . .
>
> *what if.* . . .
>
> *might have been.* . . .
>
> *could have been.* . . .
>
> *should have.* . . .
>
> *ought to have.* . . .
>
> recitative
>
> *ifonlyifonlyifonlyadinfinitum.* . . .

Most commonly these are associated with ruminations about the past, and often these clouds of dark thoughts revolve around one traumatic memory. It is as if you are trying to shake it off like a wild beast clawed to your back. To get through the awful obsessive land of the Ifonlies requires a great deal of willpower. It helps to grab each ifonly and say, "Nonsense. If I can go back and change that, then I could change all past history." An "ifonly" is a red alert which makes no sense. That is why you must remind yourself it is nonsense.

Thoughts can also float from one to another endlessly, tracking back and forth around the memory landscape of your mind. They do not let go because some magnetic power hooks onto certain memories of the past, recycling them over and over, day and night. Sometimes it is a single fixed idea. Whatever form it takes, however, it usually makes no rational sense. It is the repetition compulsion.

This futile and irrational archetypal mood is frequently associated with depression, anxiety, and panic. One actually says, "I am trapped." If one doesn't heal spontaneously—if time does not "cure" the depression, anxiety, or panic—it is a red signal to seek professional help. If the problem can't be nipped in the "but," it will spread like fire.

One must look at this image wearing the lens of "No Big Deal." You try to disentangle yourself from all of these seemingly momentous, entangling life-and-death thoughts by saying to yourself over and over again, "I am in the Forest of Trivia." And what happens to those who live this forest? They become the native Giveups who lie down and cry "uncle." The Giveups have the chronic bad habit of making all decisions

The Forest of Trivia: At the entrance to the forest, families huddle together because of the shrieking sounds of the flying monsters: the Ifonlies, Whatifs, Oughts, Mighthave-beens, Couldhavebeens, and Shouldhavebeens—all of whom fly at one out of the dark spaces.

conditionally and, once made, trying literally like the devil to undo them. To avoid being caught in the endlessly branching trees of Either This Way or That, you climb down the trunk and dig your feet into the ground. Remind yourself that whatever are the consequences of the past, you must accept the present reality as fate. In doing this, in adapting to the unchangeable present instant, the present begins to change, and at last you have a hand in the process. You are no longer trapped.

Let me tell you a little story about an ordinary fellow who lived in the City of Put . . .

William lived on the street Where You Stay. He would sit on the front porch in the evening and think and say all sorts of droll and interesting things that didn't make sense. It was as if he was talking a different language from all his friends who walked by and waved or tried to chat. One day, he could no longer stand the feeling of being out of touch with everyone and unable to reach or talk with all the people of Put (pop. 345). So he packed a bag and left the city of Put.

Down the country lane he hiked, not knowing where he was headed but knowing he had to get out of Put. In the evening, he came to an inn. A woman sat at the front desk. On the counter was her name, "Eva." Little did he know that she was the Negative Devouring Mother and the Bad Witch rolled into one Eva. She said there were no rooms for ordinary people like him, only rooms for *heroes*. He said, "What a Sad Sac am I!" and went out on the front steps and sat down in a grim, dejected mood. Along comes Adam, a Negative Father Archetype who hated Whippersnappers like Sad Sac, and began to berate him. Sad Sac was so intimidated by the Great Father that he sort of withered and the air went out of him and he was unable to speak even a word. Then he walked into the field and lay down and fell asleep.

It is hard to tell how long he slept, but it was many a summer, fall, and winter, and just as many springs. He had a dream in which Eva was the Depression Witch and snapped Sad Sac into a Whipped Whippersnapper. "If only I could be a hero, I would be all right. I would be famous."

Then a hero approached him and asked William if he would like to be *like him.* But the hero was the Faceless Famous One, and this seemed a terrible fate. William turned to Father Adam, who told him that to be a real hero was to be the Ordinary Guy That He Was. "How can I be the ordinary guy that I was?" asked William. "By staying in the city of Put on the avenue of Where You Are," said Adam.

Putnote:
This story is not true. I made it up.
But it is based on real people and real events.

To be possessed by an archetype can be illustrated by an inner voice that tells you what to think and what to do, can either torment you as a daemon or be a guardian spirit, your inner genius, or the source of your **inner dialogue.** Since this seems a superhuman unconscious voice, it can possess you with the Ifonlies, Whatifs, Oughts, Shoulds, etc. Socrates had an inner daemon that told him to play more music, which was advice for more feeling and less living in his thinking function. The daemon can be your "inner voice of conscience" or tormentor, either demonic or divine. It is an archetype of the primitive collective unconscious. In our ordinary states of mind, the daemon is the instigator of inner speech acting as our alter-ego.

Rewriting One's Own History

The World of "Ifonly"

The Gone to Crow-Caw
Gale warning!
The past is fury spinning round your head
in dizzy eerie blasts.
All the Could-Haves, Should-Haves,
Might-Haves, Would-Haves, and
Ifonlies
sing a raucous song
of the Crow Cawing.

It is called the GONE TO CROWCAW
in E-flat minor—
a haunting disharmonious cacophony
that springs at you in an
unguarded moment when the
Ifonlies fly through the forest.

A squall rustles the darkness
and I am Gone-to, but
if only I had gone the other way!
If only I had done what I ought to
have done!

If only I might have but then *what if . . . I*
had done what I ought to have done?
Then I would have what I could have
and wouldn't be in the GONE-TO
CROWING IF ONLY!
The storm subsides.
I go into the house
and batten down the windows.

"You're wise, but you lack tree smarts."

Self-Help for Depression

Advice is notoriously slippery.
People take the advice they are looking for,
and advice seekers shop for what they want to hear.

No form of human behavior prompts advice
more readily than depression.
If the depression is severe,
then well-meaning, and not-so-well-meaning,
advice givers are themselves depressing.

So, for what it's worth, here's a parcel
of thoughts and advice to give yourself.

With depression, the demons of darkness move in.
*Try to think that they will move out
when—**when**—you become master of your present fate.*

Yeah, but how do you do that?

You do it
by accepting the fate of here and now.
That is, you accept the depression.
Accept the dark thoughts and strange dreams.
Accepting is *not* the same as saying,
"Thank you. I am glad I am depressed."
If you could be *glad,* you would not
be depressed. However, in accepting your present fate,
try, if you can, to tell yourself that
however weird it seems, your depression is
serving a purpose, like fever with infection.
Tell yourself that "going through a depression"
means going down in order to come up.
Tell yourself it is just possible
that you were too "up" and needed a dose
of too "down" for a while.

A dose of too down? How in the world could that be good? How could I welcome depression?

I did not say that being too down was good.
I did not say to welcome it.
All I meant to say was "accept it."
Then you can fight it.

Do not tolerate well-wishers who tell you to,
    "Cheer up! Smile and stop being depressed!"
Because they are really talking to themselves
in your hearing. Their hidden message is,
"All you need to do is to be like me.
Don't you see, I'm not depressed because
I am cheerful, and I know how to stop
myself from being depressed."

In the psyche of the depressed person, an inner voice
may be replying in torment:
    "I know! I know! I will try! If I could, I would
    be cheerful. If I could, you damned well better
    know I wouldn't need you to tell me to stop it!"

When depression is bad, the sufferer is in the clutches of
powerful dark forces.
To tell the one in the shadow to stop it
is like telling someone to stop a tornado.
If it's coming your way, it will suck you up with all
of its destructive power,
and it would be impossible to cheer up.

Surely positive thinking is important to healing. Surely you can try to cheer up, try to tell jokes, laugh, and. . . .

Positive thinking and techniques of cheer, even having a pet,
are highly significant. I think you will see that when you come
out of your depression.

You will know better than to tell a deeply depressed
person to cheer up, smile, stand straight, and fly right.
Why?
Because you will have compassion from having been there.

Accepting your fate means:
    Depression is often a necessary corrective
    reaction to something that went wrong.
    It will force you into yourself, like into
    the storm cellar of introspection.
    You may be sad, but you will be wiser.

Can you put it in a more pithy way? I can't follow all this namby-pamby talk of depression as fate: accept it!

Yes.
For example, symptoms of depression include a sense
of diminished self-worth and a feeling
of loss of competence.
In dark times, the lights go off. Try to turn on the lights
by accepting these feelings as symptoms
that have little to do with your real self-worth
and competence.
Find ways or experiences that will reveal your worth.
Give yourself credit for what you have done that is good
and worthwhile and fight the terrible "oughts" and "shoulds"
and the torpedoes called "ifonlies."

If I give myself that kind of advice and I don't believe it, then what?

*You won't believe it at first, so try again and again
to convince yourself.*

If that won't work, then you must find someone who is truly
responsible, who is there for you,
who has no glib advice.
Seek people who will sense your inner needs
but not be so kind and nurturing that they smother you.
Many of your needs must not be met.
It is strange, but there is great meaning in suffering.

Cheap advice is counter-productive.
It engenders guilt, shame, and the ego of the giver.

I'm beginning to get you. Now you are saying that "people need people." So you have to tell someone about your inner feelings. How do you know whom to tell?

Tough question. If one is desperate and in a panic,
it seems that "any port in a storm" will do. But this is
dangerous.
Panic is often the worst part of depression, and
desperation leads to wild attempts to get high
or to desire oblivion. Depression itself is a
cry for relatedness.

Now I'm going to give you some good advice.

I thought you felt there wasn't any good advice.

No. You misunderstood, because I was saying that
most people who seek advice are seeking what they
want to hear and what they already believe.
Good advice may be the very thing they can't or won't take.

Good Advice: *Don't leak.*
By that I mean, leak to the minimum: tell about yourself,
your plight, your depression, your inner thoughts, your
dreams to as few people as possible.
By leaking, I mean talking to too many people.
The container isn't holding.
Your distress, anger, frustration, and despair
are to be revealed to few people. Very few.
Talk to as few people as possible and only to those whom
you trust and for whom you feel some love.
Close friends who have known you for a very long time
know you.
Don't tell strangers what is inside you.
Don't seek people who have or who want power over you.
Don't talk to the great-name people
because they are already inundated,
and you may end up feeling not only rejected but
affirmed in your sense of insignificance.

Sounds like a list of "don'ts."
Can't you put it in terms of "do's?"

Yes. I was going to say:
    Don't try those who pride themselves on
    their "self-made success" and have big egos.

So I will say:
    Try those who have both humility and compassion,
    who convey a sense of strength and well-being.
    Try those who will really listen to you
    and be less preoccupied with themselves.
    Try people who do not climb on other people.
    Try people who show not pity and not necessarily
    sympathy, but rather empathy.

So you talk to few people.
You contain yourself as much as possible.
You find people to be with, places to go,
things to do, and ways to keep out of bed.
Remember that
      the introverting nature of depression
      is poorly understood by extraverted
      good-old-outgoing back-slapping Americans.
      Introversion is not weakness.

Jung was the leader of what I have called the unacknowledged
Introvert Lib Movement.
Like any movement led by an introvert,
you would not expect to know anything about it.
It would be subtle and quiet—not touted.

What advice could depressed people give themselves in which they might find wisdom when faced with their most difficult problems?

Have patience.
More than anything else—have patience,
because depression usually
is a self-limited disorder. In time it will pass away.
To the sufferer, however, it seems as if it will never end.
That can play a role in suicidal ideas.
Depression does end, though.
Have patience most of all.
Time hardly moves in deep depression:
minutes drag by, anxiety overwhelms, and
agitation inhibits. Patience makes the
seemingly unbearable bearable.
Remember: "This too shall pass."
In patience dwells the soul.

I Repeat: Depression goes away.

Hold on. I know of some people who are so deeply depressed that they want to kill themselves. They try to doctor themselves and say that they do not need help. Then what?

In such situations, the depression
must be handled by a competent psychiatrist.
Medication and psychotherapy will be needed.
Sometimes hospitalization is necessary.
I knew of one patient who was on the psychoanalyst's couch

for seven years, three days a week,
being treated for an agitated depression.
When he was discharged as "analyzed,"
the depression was worse.
In some cases of depression,
analysis is contraindicated.
Uncovering depth and dream work
can only come about in other ways.

Depression is really like being at the mercy of demons
in the dungeon of despair.

In emphasizing the psychology of depression,
it must never be forgotten that
often it is essential to prescribe antidepressant medication.

I emphasize the importance of psychotherapy
and a relationship with a caring, steady human being.
The psyche is often totally ignored
by biological psychiatrists.
But then, every specialty has its own
myopic practitioners.

When Remembering Is Pain, Then Forgetting Is Happiness

But the Question Is: How to Forget?

"I never could have what I really wanted," she cried.

She tried alcohol.
It didn't work.
She became depressed.
She ruminated in dark spirits.

She tried drugs.
She became their unhappy slave:
now high, now low,
ruminating in murky, undulating moods.

She tried psychoanalysis.
Searching for *the* answer in childhood,
she ruminated endlessly, hoping
to uncover the telltale tale.
She couldn't stop her endless rumination,
so she ruminated on that.

She tried six self-help groups to feel good,
as well as six hyper-fix-charismatic workshops.
For twenty-four hours on twelve different days,
she felt good.
Then she ruminated on why the good feeling left.

She saw a psychologist and a social worker,
two psychiatrists and a Zen master.
She consulted with logicians, philosophers,
magicians, acupuncturists, mathematicians,
cognitive scientists, and neuroscientists.
Their words and ideas captivated her,
so she ruminated on their ideas.

Then one morning on a walk, she met an old woman.
All day long, they wandered down country lanes
saying nothing.
At twilight the old woman asked her,
"Where are you? You seem lost in thought.
What are you thinking?"

Everything I ever wanted I couldn't have.
Everything that would have made my life happy.
Everything that would have been wonderful slipped away.
Sometimes my father said I couldn't have it.
Sometimes my mother forbid me to take it.
Once or twice I ran away—but I came back.
I have lost all of my golden opportunities.
How sad my life has been.
All the time I am thinking. . . ."

"Don't!"

"Don't what?"

"Don't think about the time . . . when. . . .
Think about the here and now!
This present moment. Think that maybe
you have what you really sought."

"It's like a record playing in my head."

"Maybe for you, forgetting is the only medicine
for the pain you keep remembering.
You cannot forget this present instance, but
just remember that the past is illusion,
and the future never is anything
but fantasy. This 'now' is reality."

"So, when remembering is pain,
forgetting is happiness.
But the question is,
how do I forget? Tell me!"

"I forgot."

Don't tell me all dreams have a story! Some are just a mishmash of things and pieces and nothing fits in a story line. So what do you do? Manufacture a story or face the music?

A Dream Is Not to Be Taken Literally

That is Rule Number One.
There are exceptions,
but beware if you make an exception.

Simplest example: you dream of your death.
A friend tells you in panic that he dreamed he had cancer.
You dream of the death of someone whom you know.
When death dreams come out of the blue,
it almost always means something else.
Breathe easier. Dreams that foretell death
are quite different.

Of course, you can't be naive.
A woman was referred to me after dreams of going blind.
I sent her to an ophthalmologist
before I began psychologic treatment.
She had severe macular degeneration and was going blind.

If you dream of an atomic explosion,
it is more likely that you are about to experience
a dramatic upheaval
or "explosion" in your life
than that an ICBM is on the way.
Some people dream of atomic explosions
when they are dramatically getting well,
the end of another world of suffering.

The point is simple:
usually such dramatic events in dreams
are to be taken symbolically.
In short, some part of you is dying
so another part can be born or live,
or a huge wipeout is taking place.
When you dream of hanging,
you may have a hang-up you are ignoring.
I am not an admirer of a lot of clever, cute clichés,
but if the shoe fits. . . .
Yes, the unconscious is marvelous at making visual and word puns.

DREAMS

"The dream is a little hidden door in the innermost and most secret recesses of the soul, opening into that cosmic night which was psyche long before there was any ego-consciousness, and which will remain psyche no matter how far our ego-consciousness extends . . . All consciousness separates; but in dreams we put on the likeness of that more universal, truer, more eternal man dwelling in the darkness of primordial night. There he is still the whole, and the whole is in him, indistinguishable from nature and bare of all egohood. It is from these all-uniting depths that the dream arises, be it never so childish, grotesque, and immoral." Jung said that in *Civilization in Transition*. Do you agree? (Jung 1934, pp. 144-145)

Do I agree? He says man!! and all that gobbledegook about be it never so never. That's science? Maybe poetry. So what? And yet, I had a dream about such a little hidden door.

Yes and No. I don't have to agree to everything the Mahatma said. And yet, I know what he is saying because I have experienced it. Let me ponder on it: I had a dream like that.

If you dream of moving to a city
where you are contemplating moving,
it does not mean that your unconscious
is telling you to get going.
The dream is about a major move and the context
will surely be calling your attention
to something you have overlooked
in your conscious deliberation.
In a sense, dreams tell us

> —to think more

> —to use our imaginations better

> —to ignore quick and easy interpretations

> —to take our psyches seriously with a sense of humor

Your dream may cast you in a story where you are a great lover,
a great writer, a great actor, a millionaire businessperson, or
a famous person, acclaimed by great numbers of people.
BEWARE!
Look closely and think again.
It could be pulling your hubris leg.
It is more than likely a parody of your wildest fantasy.
It may be a sharp warning against a ballooning ego.

Sometimes dreams are so funny you wake up laughing
and don't even know what the joke is.
One time, when I had surgery on my left knee,
the doctor said,
"Do not sleep on your left side."
The second postoperative day, I woke up
with a sharp pain in my left knee.
I rolled over from lying on my left side, remembered my dream,
and laughed.

> *I am on a naval vessel sailing into an Egyptian harbor.*
> *A voice calls out over the squawk box:*
> *"Now hear this! This is your captain speaking:*
> *Prepare for Port Said!" [pronounced port sigh-eed]*

That was all there was to the dream.
Then it struck me.
I had not obeyed orders.
An old salt like me knows that port is left.
I had been in trouble landing on my left side.
Of course, you can make more of it if you wish,
by asking why *that* city? Why the entrance to the Suez Canal?
You can always make something out of anything.
My unconscious had come up with a wonderful one-liner.
As the song goes, "Who could ask for anything more?"

Don't abdicate your own rational mind.
Just use it to psyche out the intuitive, introverted genius
of your imagination.

Working with Dreams

We dream in periodic cycles every night. Rapid eye movement (REM) is dream sleep. The biological nature of dreaming shows in the electroencephalogram (EEG). There is a neuroscience of brain and dream.

What about the dream images and stories? Since the dream itself is soft data, most scientists don't have any truck with it. Dream interpretation is for the birds, they think. Until Freud came along, there was no powerful, systematic theory of the meaning of dreams. Next, Jung, building on Freud's dream work, developed new ways of understanding dreams.

When I was active in the San Francisco Psychoanalytic Institute in the 1950s, the classical or orthodox Freudian dogma was rigidly followed. If you didn't follow it, that meant your oedipal problem was surfacing. I would even say Freudian doctrine was followed religiously.

The remembered dream, called the manifest dream, was not important, for it was merely a disguise for a hidden or latent dream.

The theory was that the manifest dream was a censored and disguised latent dream which allowed the dreamer sleep. It was the analyst's job to ferret out the latent dream. This task was accomplished by encouraging the analysand's free associations to the manifest dream. It required brilliant mental gymnastics to figure out the real dream. So inflexible was this philosophy that the dreamer was told *not* to write down the dream. Since the psychoanalyst knew what lay behind the remembered dream, it was up to the dreamer to figure out how the analyst knew this, and once you caught on then you *ipso facto* diminished the importance of the remembered dream.

Hardly anyone believes that a dream censor works in our minds to transform latent dreams to manifest dreams so the dreamer can sleep. I

Working with dreams. . . .

doubt if many analysts warn their patients not to write down their dreams. I thought that the dream world was the most intriguing part of the psyche, since it seemed so uncontaminated by ego, coming on a hotline directly from the patient's unconscious. It was self-evident to me that dreams were meaningful. No doubt much disenchantment with dream interpretation stems from rather strange ways different therapists and analysts had and have of interpreting dreams.

We have reason to be skeptical. We do not have reason not to reason about this realm beyond ordinary logic. The dream phenomenon is so much a part of our nature that it cannot be that dreams are meaningless. Francis Crick, physicist, Nobel laureate, and the discoverer of DNA, said that dreams were like waste being processed or like garbage which should be ignored and discarded.

Since we dream off and on all night and can remember only parts of dreams (sometimes very little or none of them), how can such bits and pieces form the basis for a valid, systematic concept of the meanings of dreams?

The answers are two.

ONE: There is no systematic, valid concept of dream interpretation. Given two or three analysts, you will get two or three opinions. Even a dream analyst, all by himself, does not know the exact meaning or interpretation of a dream. There is no universal law of dream interpretation.

TWO: We can only examine what nature yields to us. Although many people are unaware or unconscious of their dreams, they can be taught to be curious and care about them. Then the odds are they begin remembering them. Even so, nobody ever remembers them all. But we must examine what we can examine and not disregard data just because they are incomplete.

Jungian psychology led me to these ideas: the manifest dream is *the dream*; it reveals more than it hides. I could approach each dream without that inner script that would inevitably lead me to prescribed ideas. I could approach each dream as a uniquely created story or set of images, then dream work becomes the most fascinating part of analysis. I could approach a dream with the reminder that I had no clear idea of its meaning until I had heard it all from the dreamer and had the dreamer's associations to the dream elements and his or her life situation at this time.

There is a reciprocal connection between the dream and the dreamer's interest in the dream. There is even a reciprocal interest between the dream and the analyst's interest in the dream (which, after all, comments on the events and people, including the therapist, in the dreamer's present life). When the dream therapist is adamant or fixed in his or her ideas, what has been called doctrinal compliance can occur.

Then Freudian analysands dream Freudian dreams, and Jungian analysands dream Jungian dreams.

People frequently consult me because of their interest in their dreams. I tell them to keep a notebook by their bedside and to write their dreams down, any time in the night. Some people prefer a small tape recorder. Don't let a single dream escape you. It often surprises me that people are not faithful in keeping their dream logs. Perhaps it slowly dawns on them that they are not so interested in their dreams after all. It also astonishes me that some people who set out to work with their dreams do not study those dreams themselves but wait for me to do it. While I may interpret this as resistance on the dreamer's part, I am more of the mind that it is laziness.

At the very least, you can write down your dreams in a dream log along with the most significant event of the preceding day, a few associations, and what you think the dream means. In other words, do your own dream laundry, dry cleaning, and pressing—the drudgery that accompanies the pleasant, airy reverie about dreams.

You said that Jungian patients dream Jungian dreams and Freudian patients dream Freudian dreams. So what's to this dream stuff anyway?

The more the analyst indulges in pure Jungian talk,
the more Jungian are the analysand's dreams.
The more archetypal books and articles
the analysands read, the more their dreams are
of Wise Old Men, Wise Old Women,
dragons, monsters, witches, visionary images. . . .

At night, the psyche processes
what the ego tried to handle during the day.
The mind awake copes with life in consciousness;
the mind asleep evokes the help of the creative unconscious.
But there is a more subtle possibility.
In such dreams, the analysand's psyche works
in unconscious compliance with what the analyst expects.
This is a sort of ESP, since the patient senses
not what is explicitly said, or read,
but what the analysand sees intuitively in the analyst's
unconscious—countertransference or repressed ideas and thoughts.

Analysts offer interpretations in rhetorical frames
to guide and initiate the patient into the system
of thought or feelings in which therapy will take place.

I discussed one of my patient's dreams with a Freudian analyst:

> *I am high on a mountain with you and I am talking*
> *to you through a large, tubelike structure. I*
> *cannot see you but can hear your voice.*
> *I feel that we are making contact but am uneasy*
> *about something.*

My colleague said he thought the dream meant
the patient was relating to me through her vagina
and wished for closer contact.
Her uneasiness meant she felt guilty
for what might happen.
The mountain was a breast and also a wish for me
to be with her.
He said it meant I should talk to her
about the sexual transference.

Despite my long Freudian training,
it never occurred to me to think
that she was relating to me through the vagina.
I do not discount her sexual fantasies, or mine,
but why interpret the large tube as a vagina?
He felt certain about his interpretation.
He even became quite excited about it,
and about how differently I saw the dream meaning.

This is how I saw her dream:
Our recent sessions had been difficult to follow
because her talking was disjointed.
She seemed to be discussing several things at the same time,
or she would start a comment but wander off
into a different area. She was scattered.
While I could determine the associations
between her various trains of thought,
it seemed to me that she needed most of all to concentrate
on how she talked to me. In other words, she needed to channel
her dialogue with me in a more direct, contained form—
that is, to get her message to me in a disciplined
manner. Of course, this would be closeness, which she avoided.
She was able to focus her insight.
The trouble was she was too high
and things weren't down-to-earth enough.

I can see. But that is a very short dream. Some of my dreams are long, and I fill pages in my dream book writing them down. I am not in therapy, so I do my own therapy, but I often wish I were in therapy so I could figure out what these long dreams mean. They are so full of detail and interesting things happening. How do you manage when someone tells you a long dream?

I try to keep it simple.
As I listen to a dream that goes on and on,
first I try to select a central theme
or some part of the dream on which to focus.
If I can't extract something simple,
I don't try to interpret the dream.
I ask the dreamer what he or she thinks it means.

If the dreamer presses me, I explain that the dream is
just too long and complicated for me to grasp.
No doubt it would end up quite unsatisfactorily
if I tried to understand it all. Worse—
I would probably find myself being verbose.

Now a word as to how you might look at long dreams.
Take a small part that is most interesting to you.
Reflect on it.
Ask yourself aloud, what could it mean?
To what inner problem is it tuned?
How is it trying to help you?

Above all, do not get bogged down
analyzing an elaborate and long dream.
That would be hard enough for the most skilled analyst,
so a little modesty please.
Do not, repeat, do not become enamored of your own long dreams.
They are probably not that great.
Rather, be thankful for having such a good feature movie
and wait for a shorter version, which is sure to follow.
Good Movie I is usually followed by Good Movie II,
or Son of Good Movie I.
Wait for the offspring.

Remember *the* dramatic highlight of a long dream.
Think about it.

Try to enjoy your dream life.
If it is unpleasant, remember:
some healing medicines taste awful.

Try to think of dreams as personal stories,
as quite good works of art.
But like a play, no matter how masterful the author
or marvelous the actors, it usually fits
into one, two, or three acts.

Some do's and some don'ts:
Don't try to understand everything.
Do try to be clear and brief.
If you can't grasp the story, make up a title for the dream.
If it is disjointed and cluttered, remember
that maybe your closet also is and you need to rummage around in it.
Do not play clever games in interpreting anyone's dream.
Do honor dreams.
Do not give clever, offhand, cookbook interpretations.
Do not play Jung or Freud.

I appeal to the natural creative spirit in everyone,
to think of your dream as a work of art.
Paint it if you can.
Dance it if you are inclined.
Embroider it if you have the patience.

While I am dreaming, it is actually happening and I can never convey how it really was. If that is the case, what's the point of going on about a cold replica of a hot dish?

I know. You know. We share this common experience.
It's like listening to a symphony in a great hall
and trying to describe it the next day.
It happened and it is over but its effect is not.
The music is the sound of the dream of the composer.

Writing about dreams is like describing a snowflake.
When the dream is happening, it is the actual dream.
When it is recalled, it is a memory of a memory.
When we write or talk about our dreams,
we, it, and the dream are changed in the process.

The dream is recycled in the retelling
and in recycling is transformed.

Still, we are always somewhat compelled
to share our wonderful experiences,

yet we can never recapture the past that is
dead and gone . . .
but rather reborn in the telling and the listening.

Is that enough?

One more word would be too much.

Great Expectations

Patient Dreams Reveal Feelings About Treatment and the Doctor

When psychotherapy or analysis just begins, the patient usually has one or more dreams that foretell extremely important expectations and unconscious judgments. Based on these, the doctor can quite reliably see how much the patient trusts him or her and the depth of the patient's commitment to the therapy process. Moreover, such a dream may yield significant clues, warnings, doubts, and admonitions about problems to be anticipated in treatment. Through the dream, the patient hears and sees an impressive message of affirmation of feeling from his or her own inner world that he or she is not ready to acknowledge or admit consciously. Confronted with these messages from himself or herself, clarified by the therapist, the patient discovers a measure of drama in the lively anticipation of what will happen in analysis.

Of course, you could challenge this concept as a self-serving one for the analyst in which the patient reads into the dream what the analyst already has thought. Such skepticism is swept away when you look at your own dream and find yourself arguing with yourself rather than the "know-it-all mind reader." Let us look at some examples.

A patient tells this dream:

I am in the catacombs of Rome where the Christians hid to avoid persecution, torture, and dismemberment. I am looking for a person who is there. I am confident that he is there. I have no fear and I am not anxious. It is dimly lit by torches here and there. I know I will do whatever is necessary to find him.

The patient's immediate association was that he was looking for his own identity and the search related to his analysis. I agreed. My inner dialogue went something like this:

"The catacombs buried under the holy city are symbolic images that stand for the personal and the collective unconscious from where the dream came. There is light, but not a lot at those depths. The catacombs were a refuge for people who were tortured for and often by their ideas, which deviated from and threatened the prevailing society, religion, and culture. Today there are skeletons in the catacombs.

"His determination to pursue his quest without fear or anxiety is good news indeed, considering his seeming skepticism and resistance to therapy during the first hour I saw him. How much of this do I tell him?"

What I actually said to him was, "The dream is a good sign of your determination to uncover and go to any dark lengths to find what you call your identity, perhaps a true identity deeply buried under the surface."

In the dream, which pleased him, he had made a heroic effort to find himself in the unconscious among martyrs. The dream has no shadow side, however. The few torches would have made some eerie shadows. The fearful shadow side of his quest appeared in his next dream, four nights later:

> I am to disarm a bomb. There are innocent people all around in obvious danger of being killed. Try as hard as I can, I am unable to disarm the bomb, and I know that sooner or later it will explode. Meanwhile, as I work on the bomb, many people escape. I feel good that they could escape because of what I was doing. All attention in the dream focuses on me. I wake up before the bomb goes off.

I said to myself:

"The 'bombshell' will go off sooner or later but it will not be as devastating as it might have been had he not gotten to work as soon as possible.

"In dreams that portend death by killing in an anonymous way like this (i.e., innocent bystanders), there is reason to think that some parts of the psyche must die or be sacrificed for other parts to live and grow, as perhaps one might prune a garden."

What I told him after this inner dialogue was that his commitment to his search for identity was not going to be without danger and unexpected things opening up, but in the dream, although he was the center of everything, he was personally in no danger, and he even woke up (became conscious) before the explosion.

Another patient had great ambitions and high intelligence plus a mixture of inflated powers, expectations, and aggression. Yet, at the same time, he had a vision of humility, of becoming a famous and humble healer of people's souls. In our second session, he related this dream:

> I am walking by some water in the woods of a resort area. I wander into an old fisherman's shack. The old man has gone away. The shack has a lot of fishing equipment that the fisherman sells. I decide that since [he] has gone away, I will move into his shack and take over the business. I go to the counter and realize that I don't have any change, so it would be difficult to sell . . . anything. I set myself up as the proprietor. Then a doctor and his wife come in. The doctor turns on a light and says, "Let me help you."

The dreamer associates the doctor and wife with me and my wife, and with me bringing light and the offer to help. The old fisherman who had left he called the Wise Old Man. It seemed to me that this was an extraordinary cue that, in its depth, his psyche had helping and serving powers that were going to take over, given this opportunity in the woods of the dream. The fisherman's disappearance was followed by the appearance of the helper/doctor as if one had come back in the guise of the other. But the patient was not ready for this move. There wasn't yet enough change.

I told him that it was a positive dream about where his therapy might lead. I reminded him that there was nothing grand about the fisherman's shack. I did not want to appear too insightful or clever at this early stage of our relationship. Somewhere Jung wrote that to be always understood by the doctor is a terrible thing. While this patient had a significant problem with trust, he was allowing me in.

A Sure-Fire Dream Interpretation When "Bad News" Equals "Good News"

An actor preparing for a performance, a speaker who will give a lecture, a student facing an examination, a person about to undertake a difficult or frightening task or commitment that will test his or her character or training is, in short, a person who faces an ordeal feeling great apprehension or anxiety. Having carefully and deliberately prepared for the event, he or she will nonetheless have a dream of bad news, but which is really good news.

Freudians call this kind of dream a "matriculation dream." In Jungian parlance, it would represent an initiation or threshold archetype. It is the kind of dream that can be interpreted with almost 99 percent certainty to have the opposite meaning from the apparent one.

It is so predictable that I never hesitate to make a flat-footed interpretation of impending success. A typical illustration would be a diligent student who dreams of failing an examination in disgrace only to pass the exam the next day with honors.

A real life example:

A man whose life was dominated by high achievement and a driving ambition for recognition and fame came to see me because of dreams that frightened him just at the time when he achieved his life's dream, a position of great importance. When he was beginning his job, the idea of failure, of not fulfilling people's high expectations of him, almost panicked him. He thought that he might have been good before he reached his goal, but now surely he would fall from this pinnacle. He called himself stupid, dumb, a hoax. None of these insults were even remotely true. He just knew he would fail. He made an appointment with me and then he had this dream:

I am in a big auditorium full of people who are waiting for the show to begin. I am behind the curtain frantically rushing around to find something at the last minute before the curtain goes up. Someone calls, "Curtain time!" I have stage fright. Then there appears a man at my side whose expression is one of indifference. As the curtain rises, this other man grabs the curtain and goes up with it, hanging on with his hands. He won't let loose because he would fall, and it is obvious that he is just barely holding on. The performance is about to begin, and I am not in it, although in a way I am it. I quickly fall to the floor so as not to be conspicuous and hold my hands over my eyes, like a child playing peek-a-boo, with the fingers of one hand spread so I can see both the audience and the performance. I am aware that the audience can see both me and the man hanging onto

the curtain, but they pay no attention to either of us. In fact, they ignore us. They are keeping their eyes on the performance.
In the dream, I think that there is something funny about the man hanging on the curtain and myself crouching on the floor like a child half hiding my eyes. Then, I feel fear and wake up.

This man is hanging on desperately, yet trying to get out of the picture. He is split into another part of himself, the child who tries to hide yet see the whole performance at the same time. The "audience," his grown-up observers, pay no attention to the peripheral goings on, only to the show that has begun. The dreamer has no fear that there will be anything wrong with the show; he is just trying to keep out of the limelight. He can't do that. Since he thought that maybe he was the show, one could say that everything was proceeding according to schedule, including the two funny people trying to remain inconspicuous on stage. But it was his dream, his show. Nothing would stop it now.

I assured him that the dream meant that he had a deep sense of confidence that his preparations for the job would be successful, and there was no way to hide from that. His "hang-up" is the ubiquitous phobia high achievers have of failure, stupidity, and not being able to do what they are really excellently and well trained to do.

He was bewildered by my interpretation because he had thought the dream meant that as soon as the curtain rose, he would fall on his face and try to cover his shame. But his psyche had a sense of humor, saying, "Yeah, you will fail. Like this, you will fail." And the show went on. In the dream, however, he is no famous star. This image is compensation for hubris keeps him low. This helpful dream got us off to a good start, because his performance at work was successful and acclaimed.

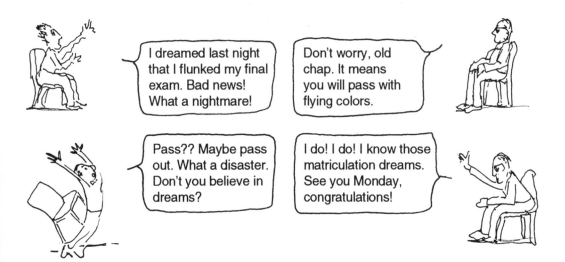

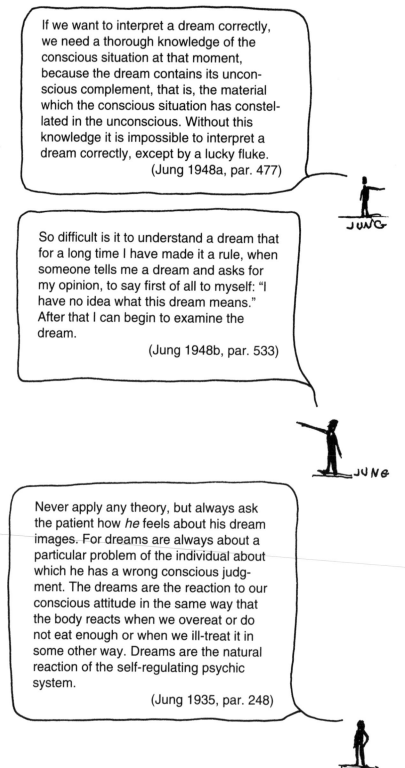

If we want to interpret a dream correctly, we need a thorough knowledge of the conscious situation at that moment, because the dream contains its unconscious complement, that is, the material which the conscious situation has constellated in the unconscious. Without this knowledge it is impossible to interpret a dream correctly, except by a lucky fluke.
(Jung 1948a, par. 477)

JUNG

So difficult is it to understand a dream that for a long time I have made it a rule, when someone tells me a dream and asks for my opinion, to say first of all to myself: "I have no idea what this dream means." After that I can begin to examine the dream.
(Jung 1948b, par. 533)

JUNG

Never apply any theory, but always ask the patient how *he* feels about his dream images. For dreams are always about a particular problem of the individual about which he has a wrong conscious judgment. The dreams are the reaction to our conscious attitude in the same way that the body reacts when we overeat or do not eat enough or when we ill-treat it in some other way. Dreams are the natural reaction of the self-regulating psychic system.
(Jung 1935, par. 248)

JUNG

A Dream About Mortality

WOMAN: I want to tell you the dream I had this morning.
            I am working on a ward for AIDS patients.
            There are about twenty men dying.
            Suddenly I notice
                a lesion of some sort on my finger.
            When I touch my body, The Disease spreads.
                I realize that I have AIDS.

            Purple spots spread over my entire body.
            I wonder—
                "When will the pain come?"
            The pain that means the end stage of AIDS.

            But one thing I do know:
            I will keep on nursing and helping
                on this ward as long as I can.

        This is a dream about death.

WILMER: This is a dream about AIDS.
            What do you think about AIDS?

WOMAN: . . . I feel . . . deep down I feel that
            if you get involved with sex
                that you get punished,
            and at my stage of life, getting older,
            these old teachings about sex still haunt me.
            You know
                I am very judgmental.
            You know
                I don't want anyone to touch me.

WILMER: You said this dream was about death.

WOMAN: It was as if I smelled mortality.

WILMER: I see.
                You were afflicted with AIDS.
                And by touching your own body,
                you were causing it to spread.
                What does that mean to you?

WOMAN: I think
I am more afraid of touching myself—
maybe even like being in touch with myself—
that part of me that
is aware of my own mortality.
I don't want to come near to *that.*

WILMER: Apparently you must do just that
which you fear. . . .
You are determined to keep in touch with
the men dying of AIDS.
Why is that?

WOMAN: In the dream, I feel their loneliness,
their isolation,
their fear and dread,
their hope and their hopelessness,
their suffering,
because of my very judgmental attitude.
I know some homosexuals,
but homosexuality doesn't touch my life
except
in a symbolic way.

WILMER: What do you mean, "except in a symbolic way"?

WOMAN: Like my concern with being a nurse, a healer
on a ward devoted entirely to AIDS patients.
And even though I have AIDS. . . . . .
Now that I hear myself saying that,
I realize that I am dying of AIDS, and
I myself belong on that ward.
A woman with AIDS.

WILMER: You do identify with the men.
You want to make amends for your dark feelings.
You are sensitive to touching as if
it were a deadly matter.
[lost in thought about himself, he then returns to her]
How did you feel while you were dreaming?

WOMAN: Apprehensive . . .
You see, I was waiting for The Pain.
The signal of the coming end.

WILMER: Why do you call it The Pain?

WOMAN: Because, as I said,
       It is the omen of death.
       It is the pain of recognition of mortality.

WILMER: I see.
       We all face death sooner or later.
       Why do you suppose you dreamt that this morning—
       Nursing men with AIDS?

WOMAN: Yes, nursing, but I felt like I was doctoring.
       Like you. I was anticipating seeing you today.
       Maybe because I want to do what you do,
       like working with AIDS patients.
       I don't mean *really,* but . . .

WILMER: But symbolically, like you do in the dream.
       Perhaps the dream means that you need to
       care for yourself, be both nurse and doctor,
       man and woman.

WOMAN: That feels right. I understand.

WILMER: You are tending to that self that is hurt,
       which is in isolation, suffering.
       You are helping to create a special place,
       a safe place where that part can die.
       When we dream such dreams, it is not
       specifically about our death, or even
       our contracting the sickness, but
       that a part of us must die
       so that another part can live.

WOMAN: I suppose it is like death and rebirth,
       destruction and creation.

WILMER: What more dramatic, more provocative example
       could your unconscious have given you
       of the urgency, the life-and-death immediacy,
       to face some darkness. It is shown
       in the guise of your own mortality,
       and your own role in responsibility both
       for destruction and healing.

WOMAN: Does that mean you are the doctor on the ward?

WILMER: Not really. Not even in the dream.
>   There is a "generic doctor" somewhere in the dream
>   and that is what you see. You project onto me.
>   But it is your inner nurse and physician.
>>   You are nursing and doctoring, not I.
>>   It is your prejudice about sex,
>>   and the collective prejudice
>>   that dramatizes your problem
>>   in a hospital ward.
>   It is not only your need to be in touch with yourself,
>   but to be in touch with people.
>   In the dream, you dread this touch
>>   as if it were the kiss of death.
>   Does that seem right to you?

WOMAN: Yes.
>   But there is fear in the dream of The Pain,
>   of apprehension when it would come.
>   What do you make of that?

WILMER: That maybe it has come.
>   That maybe the pain you are now suffering
>   is The Pain for which you have been waiting.
>   And your common humanity transcends deepest fears
>>   in a symbolic way.
>   The way of pain is also the way of healing.
>   Pain, too, is a harbinger and warning of something
>>   deeper.
>   All healers are in need of healing.
>   You know the old adage, "Physician, heal thyself."
>   In Jungian psychology, that is the archetype of
>   the Wounded Healer,
>   and it is woundedness and healing oneself
>   that gives us the power to heal others.

WOMAN: Didn't Jung once say that the doctor can't go any further
with the patient than he has gone with himself?

WILMER: Yes. You know.
The dream is not about your death in reality,
but your fear of death,
your living in fear of touching and closeness.
If we live in fear of dying, we are not really living.
The dream suggests that there is "no cure"
in the sense that the task of healing oneself
is a lifelong daily task to the very end—
that is, until we die.
And if we are really living that way until we die,
we are not suffering the hopelessness you are
combating in your dream.
Perhaps I have said too much.

WOMAN: No . . . I know that I don't have to worry personally
about AIDS.

WILMER: Except . . . in a symbolic way,
in that such an affliction touches everyone
in some way.

WOMAN: [long pause] Yes, I suppose so. [long pause again]

WILMER: What were you thinking?

WOMAN: What I didn't want to tell you: I told this dream
to my Freudian friend.
He said that it meant that my unconscious feelings
and memories of masturbation, you know,
"touching myself,"
were associated with childhood guilt.
He pointed out that there was NO doctor on the ward,
and that my wanting to be like you
was a *fatal Electra complex.*

WILMER: Do you think so?

WOMAN: No, and even if there is a grain of truth in it,
          what good does it do me to focus on that?

WILMER: Did you ask your friend?

WOMAN: No, because it didn't make any sense to me.
          I prefer to think that part of the dream
          speaks to a kind of devotion or dedication
          to the healing task,
                    and the need to know the pain
                    that, as you say, I already have,
                    and not to fear the pain I do not have.
          (pause)
          In other words,
          the fear of dying is the fear of living.

WILMER: Precisely.

> Dreams prepare, announce, or even warn about certain situations,
> often long before they actually happen. This is not necessarily a
> miracle or a precognition. Most crises or dangerous situations have a
> long incubation, only the conscious mind is not aware of it. Dreams
> can betray the secret. They often do, but just as often, it seems, they
> do not. Therefore our assumption of a benevolent hand restraining us
> in time is doubtful. Or, to put it more positively, it seems that a benev-
> olent agency is at work sometimes but at other times not. The mysteri-
> ous finger may even point the way to perdition. One cannot afford to
> be naive in dealing with dreams. They originate in a spirit that is not
> quite human, but is rather the breath of nature—of the beautiful and
> the generous as well as the cruel goddess. If we want to characterize
> this spirit, we would do better to turn to the ancient mythologies and
> the fables of the primeval forest. Civilization is a most expensive process
> and its acquisitions have been paid for by enormous losses, the extent
> of which we have largely forgotten or have never appreciated.
>
> (Jung 1961, par. 473)

JUNG

Dream as Hodge-Podge of Fragments

When Is a Dream Narrative Only a Contrived Story?

Sometimes we wake up with a strange bunch of pieces of dreams, unrelated images, vignettes, segments of stories, and meandering, rambling stuff floating in our minds. To try to weave these fragments into a narrative would be a clever bit of mental gymnastics. Of course, one can do that, but what's the point?

Now you are talking sense. Perhaps they are all related to eating cabbage and drinking Irish coffee the night before. Those dream yarns you have been telling me are pretty convincing, but how do we account for the mishmash dream?

Can you tell me such a dream?

Yes, but I don't call it a dream because it is just a bunch of meaningless pictures and episodes:

> *I am pointing my finger at someone,*
> *and he becomes very small.*
> *Then I see an eye*
> *floating in space, and it frightens me*
> *and I wake up. Then I go back to sleep*
> *and see a man riding a horse and somewhere else,*
> *a man is laughing. He opens his mouth very*
> *wide and shouts and screams. A man is riding*
> *on a dog and his head becomes a hand.*
> *There is a series of images that don't hang*
> *together, a dog with a rag in its mouth,*
> *a dancing lady holding a huge broom,*
> *a belly dancer, and a man*
> *juggling heads growing another head himself.*

I see. I mean I don't see anything more than a lot of disjointed pictures. There is a sequence in which they occur and it makes a bizarre, surrealist canvas.

There you go making something out of nothing—a surrealistic canvas. Is that supposed to be a work of art?

In a way, I suppose you might say that: like a sloppy canvas or sketches to be made into a picture.

I have a rule of thumb:

> Think of nonnarrative dreams as if
> you were listening to a symphony
> playing "Pictures at an Exhibition,"
> as if the dream were a musical romp
> through a very strange gallery.

> Or imagine that, instead of music,
> the fragments are paintings on the wall,
> and each one comes to life
> as you pass it.
> It makes no difference which way you go
> through the gallery
> because the pictures are only
> animated when you stand before them.

> The same assortment can been seen
> as the pages of a small photograph album
> turning.

> You don't have to try to spin a yarn.
> But it might be wise to note the images
> and to see how or if they appear
> in subsequent, coherent dreams.
> You would be wise to think that the mishmash dream
> is a kind of workshop and rehearsal
> for a coming event
> in the Theater of Dreams.

I knew you would have some answer. Doesn't anything I ever ask stump you?

I don't know.

Dreams Are Meaningless

Don't Waste Your Time Fooling With Them

Dialogue with a Man:

MAN: My psychiatrist doesn't want to work with my dreams. He doesn't think they are important. He says that is the current attitude in psychiatry. Not only is there less interest in dreams, but also in psychotherapy. He sees me now once a month for fifteen minutes to refill my desiprimine. Why does he say that dreams are not important?

WILMER: I think that is his truth. There is no point in working with dreams with a therapist who doesn't think the dream is significant. But did you ask him why he doesn't think dreams are important?

MAN: He says that he had some training in psychoanalysis, but that even psychoanalysts are less interested in dreams than they were. And he found that working with patients' dreams was useless.

WILMER: Well, what do *you* think?

MAN: I think my dreams are very interesting and important.

WILMER: Then find a therapist who likes to work with dreams. This may not be the best analogy, but suppose your mechanic is excellent at repairing any kind of automobile, yet he doesn't like to work on Mercedes. You wouldn't take your Mercedes to him.

MAN: I don't have a Mercedes. I have a Cougar.

WILMER: You wouldn't take your Cougar to a veterinarian. And you wouldn't take your child to a geriatric physician.

MAN: Well, once, in the past, I discussed my dreams with a psychoanalyst, but I thought his interpretations were far out in space or just plain wrong.

WILMER: Did you tell him that?

MAN: No.

WILMER: Then you weren't in analysis. You were just seeing an analyst. Not everyone who works with dreams is skilled in doing this. It is both an art and a discipline. In a way, unfortunately, you have to take your chances.

MAN: That's like buying a pig in a poke.

WILMER: Not quite, but sometimes almost.

Dialogue with a Woman:

WOMAN: I would like to talk to you about my dreams, because it seems to me that a doctor who says dreams are unimportant is just ignorant. To find the meaning, that's something else. I have many dreams that don't make sense to me because dreams can be interpreted in so many different ways, yet, I have dreams that are so vivid, so remarkable that I can't forget them. How do I know what is the *right* interpretation?

WILMER: Easy. There is *no* right interpretation. But there are wrong interpretations. Some right interpretations are more right than others, and the ones most right seem to click cleanly as if they had suddenly matched some deep knowledge and wisdom that was in your mind. They "click" like the right key opening a treasure box where you can see what has been in your own mind all the time. The problem is that the dream key maker also has to be skilled in the art. The scientists in the dream research laboratories give us vital information on the process of dreaming, but they don't and can't tell us the meanings of dreams.

WOMAN: As I said at the start, I want to tell you one of my dreams.

WILMER: Why don't you work with your own dreams?

WOMAN: By myself?

WILMER: Why not?

WOMAN: Isn't that dangerous? Isn't a little knowledge a dangerous thing? Wouldn't that be like doing my own dentistry?

WILMER: Not at all. Since you obviously remember your dreams and are curious about them, I would be stupid to tell you, "Don't try to figure out your own dreams." I would be inferring that you must be an analyst or that you are sorta dumb. Sure, you can make a stupid interpretation. You can be stupid in anything. Don't try to understand your dreams with cookbook recipes (i.e., this always means that to make a batch of the other). Instead, respect and honor your dreams by stewing in the dream to see what comes out. I grant you that if you were talking to an analyst who knew you and your life and dreams, together you would do a better job than you could do alone. The analyst would see things that you didn't see and put the dreams into a perspective that you had not thought of. Moreover, merely telling your dreams to someone who really listens is itself healing. Since this is the first time I have ever seen you, I prefer not to interpret your dream now. You need to discover your associations to your dream and talk about your life at the time of the dream.

WOMAN: I have a trunk full of dreams! Maybe I'm a dream junkie. I suppose my trunk is a treasure chest. You know, talking with you makes me think that what is important is the dream of last night. That most of all. And those powerful, unforgettable, big dreams. Maybe if I work at my dreams by myself, I could find someone to talk them over with when I am perplexed and think there is some valuable insight I don't get.

WILMER: Yes. But write down your dreams immediately when you wake up or when you first remember the dream. Keep the dreams in a notebook and date each dream. Write out what you think it means. If you take that trouble, you might be surprised at what you can see. But don't fall in love with your words. Just remember that the main problem in self-analysis is counter-transference.

SEVEN

When Analysis Begins, You Can Count on the Shadow Rearing Its Ugly Head

A First Dream: A Dark Shadow

A depressed, high-risk, suicidal patient consulted me. She poured out her sad and tragic story. She told me that she kept a stash of sleeping pills that she had been saving from various doctors' prescriptions. She said she would come back and talk to me once more. I told her to bring the pills when she came or not to come. She berated her husband, men in general, and me in particular and walked out in sullen anger, saying she would never give up the drugs and that her wish to kill herself was part of the depression for which she came to me to be treated. She had been depressed and suicidal for several years and was full of vituperation for her husband's behavior. She had reasons for her anger against him, but she didn't want to give him up either. To work with me, she had to give up something. It would be her lethal secret store of drugs acquired from doctors who had tried to help her or doctors who prescribed drugs rather than listened.

At the very end of our first hour, she told me a dream which she had the previous night in anticipation of coming to see me:

> *I am in a tomb. There are two steel doors, one on my right and one on my left. There is tremendous pressure behind each door. It is so great that the doors bulge in as if they will burst. In the center of the tomb is a skeleton with a very old and shabby dress partly covering it. The skeleton is sitting in a rocking chair.*

I made no interpretation. I made no comments on the dream. I thought I knew exactly what it meant on the most important level—an urgent, even emergency message to me. I gave her an appointment to come back the next afternoon and bid her goodbye (with considerable apprehension). I knew that many of my colleagues would have rushed to get her committed or, in fear of being sued, would have called her family or even her husband. I figured there was a fifty-fifty chance she would come back the next day with the pills. Two hours later, the secretary brought me a large envelope. I was surprised to find in it the pills I had demanded as a condition of seeing the patient. Things were moving fast, but the dream said to go very slowly.

My inner dialogue continued off and on until I saw her. Do you press the idea of hospitalization? Do you dig into the suicidal ideas and evaluate for the record the risk and your own judgment? Do you interpret the dream? No. Don't do any of those things. Why not? Because her dream tells you the depth of her darkness, how close she feels to death and the tomb, how imprisoned her depression makes her, and that the danger in the dream is the pressure behind the doors. Oh! I see. So don't open any doors. No bravery. No interpretation of the dream. She surely let off some steam from her boiler room by indicating quickly she wanted to see me enough to comply with my common-sense edict. Surely she got the message "NO!" and surely there was a chance of seeing what had died in her and what the old skeleton meant to her. The steel doors were still holding. I read the dream as meaning to go exceedingly slowly in her therapy. Don't press! Don't push. Just let her come and talk. And so she did.

I prescribed antidepressant medication for her, but the main thing that happened was that our relationship developed and she found a calmness that would be her oxygen. About twenty years have passed since then. She never tried to commit suicide. She left her husband. She got a job. Once a year or so she calls me up to say how well she is doing. The dream that guided me in her analysis? I don't recall if I ever mentioned it to her.

Drawing a Shadow Dream

Visualizing a dream is an aid toward comprehending it. Drawing a dream helps fix the images in memory.
With the story reduced to minimal number of explicit images, we can build a dream story using the images as scaffolding.

Just begin to draw and don't worry about being an artist or having talent. Everyone can sketch with lines, and arrows, figures of people or things, a word or quote here and there. Bring the static figures into action by lines, and swirls or number the sequences. Remember if a child can draw, you can draw. It is not for exhibition.

Writing down the dream is the first step.
Then make the sketch.
If you are interested in another person's dream
(whether as a therapist, friend, or listener),
drawing it will be a bridge between the two of you.
You can get the dreamer to make corrections.

Rule of Thumb

First, try to see sequential dreams that occur the same night as two parts of the same story. Most often this will seem right and make sense, since the two parts follow in time sequence as an association. Imagine that the first part is the essence of the dream, and the second part is a symbolic or explicit elaboration or *denouement* holding the key meaning of the dream as if it were a statement.

Get the picture right
on hearing the dream.
If you can't talk with the dreamer,
you might be thinking about a dream image
in your head.

" In the dream I was
walking up to a big house..."

If you draw the dream images and check it out with the dreamer,
the house you imagine on a hill at night
might actually be a smaller house in the meadow
in the early morning.

Sketches of a dream drawn as the dreamer told me her dream. The four sequences were drawn on one ordinary sheet of paper, then cut apart and placed in the "story board" monitors to emphasize the images as "seen" by me and later clarified in discussion with the dreamer.

1

Part I: Sunday dream in which a tornado moves toward the dreamer's house as the dreamer is about to get married. She writes about this in her autobiography which is a "co-authored book." Somehow the wind dies down and she is safe.

Part II: She is being driven in a car by a man who seems drained of life, pale, and like a ghost. It is night and they are going very fast.

3

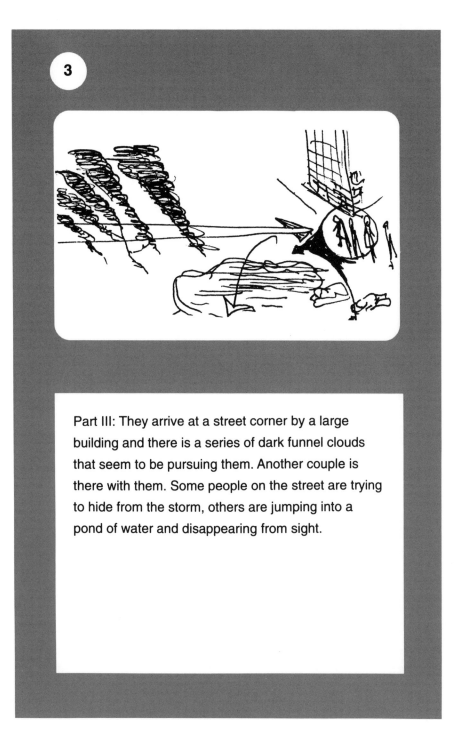

Part III: They arrive at a street corner by a large building and there is a series of dark funnel clouds that seem to be pursuing them. Another couple is there with them. Some people on the street are trying to hide from the storm, others are jumping into a pond of water and disappearing from sight.

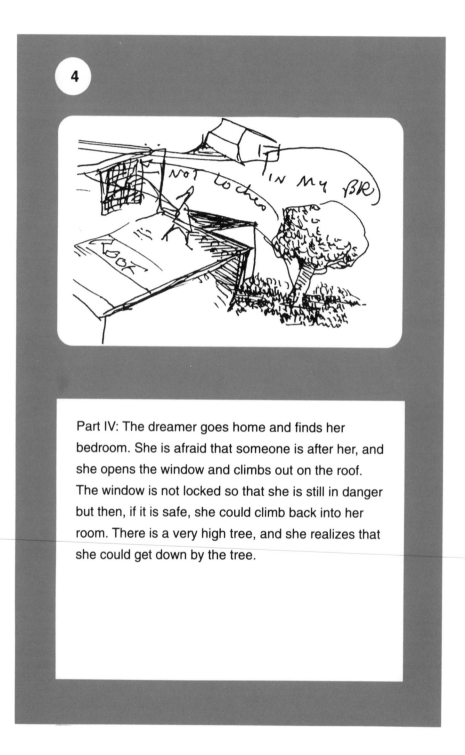

Part IV: The dreamer goes home and finds her bedroom. She is afraid that someone is after her, and she opens the window and climbs out on the roof. The window is not locked so that she is still in danger but then, if it is safe, she could climb back into her room. There is a very high tree, and she realizes that she could get down by the tree.

B

Dreamer: Last night, before the dream, I had a big fight with my fiancé, you know we are going to get married in five weeks. He just won't listen to me when I try to tell him that I am making a terrible mistake and that there is nothing I can do about it. I am trapped. There is no way out. But the dream shows that, in the end, I can get back in or out if I want to. So I felt good when I woke up, but who is the ghostly pale man and why does the tornado follow me? I don't know what the dream is telling me to do.

Therapist: The dream is not telling you what to do. It is showing you that you are writing an autobiography with a co-author! There is a big storm blowing your fears and feelings. The ghostly man who is driving you away is the pallid men who haunt you, and you are carried away by them. It leads to an intersection. Now you are calm, even in the face of multiple tornadoes. To hide, jump headfirst into the unconscious, is where panic leads. In the end, there is your bedroom and you are afraid, but you can get out, or come back in. And there is a way to get back on the ground. A tree!

Sketching Your Dreams

Fixing Them in Your Conscious Memory Bin: A Little Imagination Here, A Little Imagination There

I drew this picture as a patient told me her dream. I have no trouble remembering it. I think I remember it better than the patient. She asked to see my sketch and then began drawing and remembering her dreams better than I did. That is the way it is supposed to be.

> *Dream:*
> *A friend of mine is a mean police officer, and she is cruel to prisoners in the jail. Her boss is standing behind her and angry that she is brutal to the prisoners. He is looking daggers at her but doing nothing and saying nothing. I am an observer behind her boss, and I am outraged at my friend's behavior. But I don't do anything, and I don't think I am supposed to do anything, yet I have feelings of anger that my good friend could behave like that.*

Two-part dream of the policewoman and the jail scene, and the space trip to the terrifying planet with the decapitated head on the lab table.

Then the dream changes and I am in a rocket exploring outer space. At first, I come to a terrifying planet. I know there is great danger there and cruel people on it. I escape and fly to other planets (which are dangerous) to be explored, but I am drawn back to the terrifying planet. When I land, I go into an experimental laboratory, and I am horrified to see a dead head on the lab table.

We will not discuss her life but rather the dream which indicated to her that she had to make some observations in her shadow world of a cruel friend (her shadow) and a dream man who has authority over her but does not exert it. This is a picture of the world and the police as bullies. The law-and-order people are not right. With this prelude of the jail (who is the prisoner?), we next see the story amplified in space—journey to a terrifying place to which she is inevitably drawn away from safe explorations. She rockets to this image of an experimental research laboratory where a head is being examined. She says this is her analysis. She has a major shadow problem, and because she tried to belittle it and ignore it consciously, her dream gives her the message in an inescapable manner.

She can hardly ignore the focus of attention in the dream. Only by "facing it" will it lose its power. Her final comment, with a kind of laugh, was to say that it was a "far-out dream" and that she didn't want to think of herself as "a dead head." That was an encouraging twist after the initial look.

The dream suggests that she needs to explore the cruel jailer within her and also the masculine boss side who hates her but tolerates and supports her behavior. There is, however, another woman watching, whose conscience expresses disgust. It would seem that the dreamer is not really aware of her own shadow. The other part of her feminine self makes her aware, however.

The problem presented in the dramatic scene above is now explored in a second part that comes to a sharp focus at the end.

A new version of cruelty and terror is enacted in a rocketship saga. Once the space mission begins, it has a life of its own that cannot be escaped. There is no safe "out." Irresistible forces draw the dreamer to come face to face with the outcome of an experiment she did not want to see. This isolated, decapitated head calls attention to the place of reason that is disconnected from feeling.

You might think of the "camera work" as slowly and inexorably bringing into sharp relief the symbolic ending of the scenario.

Perhaps it is calling attention to the uselessness of the rational, logical approach to her troubled spirit and soul, which, being disconnected, suggests the need for balance of both for healing or wholeness.

Check one of the following:

True	False	The Question
☐	☐	The head on the table means loss of power, like castration. Since you didn't tell us the sex of the head, it looks like this is what she would like to do to her boss, or even to you.
☐	☐	Since a head is, after all, sexless, there being no body, this dream could point out the danger of losing one's head or mind in a horrible place.
☐	☐	Jail means containment. Handcuffs and punishment mean the justified treatment for a man who is a captured criminal. The rocket ship is her penis that projects her through space. It is power and penetration. Thus, this is an Electra complex dream.
☐	☐	This is the story of Athena, a war goddess and the virgin goddess of women, liable to violent wrath. It is a dream of horror of the patriarchal sexist society. Labor/atory means giving birth to a new idea.
☐	☐	It demonstrates the uselessness of drawing dreams.
☐	☐	It demonstrates the meaninglessness of dream interpretation.
☐	☐	None of the above.
☐	☐	I want to speak to my analyst before committing myself.

Let Us Have Your Interpretation of a Dream

This part is an exercise of your imaginative powers. There is no right interpretation. Remember that! Without knowing the patient's history and what was transpiring in the dreamer's life at the time of the dream, an interpretation is only an experience in clear thinking and intuition.

Read the following dream very carefully. If you only have time to skim it, forget it! Otherwise, write what you think about it. What comes out of it will tell you much about yourself because with the meager information I have given you, you will inevitably look at the dream as if it were your own.

After writing down your thoughts about the dream, read the questions I have asked following the dream.

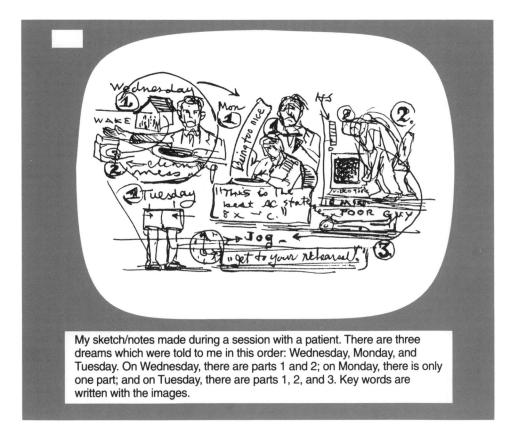

My sketch/notes made during a session with a patient. There are three dreams which were told to me in this order: Wednesday, Monday, and Tuesday. On Wednesday, there are parts 1 and 2; on Monday, there is only one part; and on Tuesday, there are parts 1, 2, and 3. Key words are written with the images.

Part I: I am standing against a wall where I know I am about to be executed. I ask the leader of the execution squad to let me go for a few minutes as I have something very important to do before the execution.

Part II: He lets me go. I run and run across the countryside until I come to a building. I am going up and down stairs until I can find your office, Dr. Wilmer. There, waiting for me outside your office, is the executioner.

Part III: I rush past him and burst into your office. You are sitting behind an enormous black desk. Across the front of the desk, chess figures are arranged like a picket fence. The King and Queen are at one end, and the pawns are at the other.

Part IV: I say to you, "Dr. Wilmer, I want to tell you something!" You reply, "Do you have an appointment? You can't tell me anything

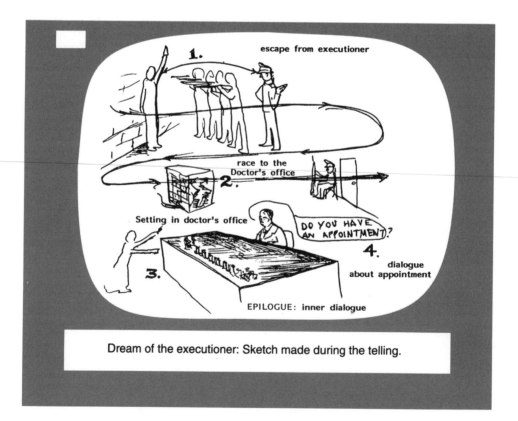

Dream of the executioner: Sketch made during the telling.

unless you have an appointment." I respond, "I don't have an appointment," and thinking to myself that it would take me no more time to tell you that I am not afraid than it would take to talk to you about the appointment.

Epilogue: I wake up cheerful, thinking that I had not told you the news that I was not afraid and that I had not been executed.

Do not read below this line unless you have finished writing about the dream.

Questions (and some answers):

1. If you think of Part I of the dream as a prologue that sets the stage for the drama that follows, then the rest of the dream would be commentary on the opening scene. It could then follow that Part II is the quest for the place to find out, and Part III is the symbolic confrontation while Part IV is an answer in the koanlike* dialogue between the patient and the doctor, the student and the guru. In this frame of mind, an enlightenment comes to the student/patient without help. Then the epilogue, in its affect and its message, gives an interpretation whose deeper meaning would go back to understanding what the execution meant.

2. If you think of the dream as an escape from death at the hands of a masculine firing squad, the frantic search for a father who sits behind a fence of chess players on a big black desk, you come to an entirely different set of feelings and meanings. When the dream is set in those terms, the doctor's response becomes officious, rigid, and uncaring or

---

Koan: A short story given by a Zen master to a monk or Zen Buddhist student to meditate upon, which (when comprehended) leads to enlightenment. These Zen stories, called *koans*, are illogical commentaries handed down over generations. The word literally means a "public document" (*kung-an*) when it is used to test the genuineness of the student's enlightenment. Koans are sometimes called "complications" (*ke-t eng*)—literally meaning "vines and wisteria," which are intertwining and entangling. According to the masters, there ought not to be any such thing as a koan in the very nature of Zen, since the truth of Zen has no need for koans (Suzuki 1961, pp. 255, 333).

Example of a koan: Someone asked the master, "Summer comes, winter comes. How shall we escape from that?"

The master answered, "Why not go to the place where there is neither summer nor winter?"

"Where can such a place be found?" asked the enquirer.

The master replied, "When winter comes it is cold. When summer comes it is hot" (Suzuki 1972, p. 90).

perhaps demanding of obedience to his rules and patterns of conduct. In other words, he is not really "with you" but hides behind rituals of kings and queens and pawns. And then who gets the last laugh?

3. If you think of the dream as an oedipal dream, then you can put everything into that Procrustean bed.

4. If you think of this as the life and death journey to the Great Father archetype, then you can put everything into that Procrustean bed.

Please finish the following sentences for your own set of ideas:

A. If you think of the dream in the frame of. . . . .

B. Then Part I suggests. . . . . .

C. And it follows that Parts II and III mean. . . . . . .

D. So that the wrapup in Part IV says. . . . . .

E. The Epilogue is a (paradoxical) commentary that says. . . . . . .

F. I would give the dream this title. . . . .

Check One:

☐   This dream is pure nonsense.
☐   This dream is a beautiful archetypal journey.
☐   This dream confirms Freudian oedipal complex.
☐   This dream has been messed up by you dividing it and pretending it is a play or a story.
☐   This dream is a pun on a picket fence.
☐   This dream is a premonition of a coming, potentially fatal, event.
☐   This dream shows the patient's overdependency on the analyst.
☐   This dream shows that the analyst and the executioner are the same.
☐   This dream is a warning to get out of analysis before it is too late.
☐   This dream cannot be understood as anything but an exercise in how many different ways there are to approach a dream and can only be interpreted if one knows the patient's associations.
☐   You are a dummy. Was the dreamer a man or a woman, or don't you believe in sex?
☐   None of the above.

"How Many Dreams Do You Have?"

"How Many Dreams Can You Remember?"

"Why Don't I Remember My Dreams?"

"Next Time I'll Have a Lot of Dreams!"

"I Only Have One Dream to Tell You."

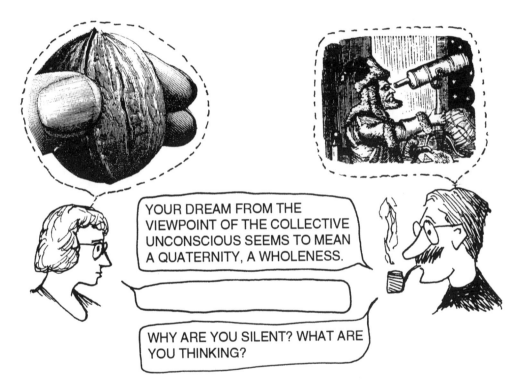

YOUR DREAM FROM THE VIEWPOINT OF THE COLLECTIVE UNCONSCIOUS SEEMS TO MEAN A QUATERNITY, A WHOLENESS.

WHY ARE YOU SILENT? WHAT ARE YOU THINKING?

ANSWERS

You need only one dream!
Don't worry about bringing a lot of dreams.
It's not the quantity that counts.
It's not how involved and "wonderful" they are.
You will remember your dreams when you need them.
You must work at your dreams, however.

A CONVERSATION

DREAMER: I can't remember my dreams. I had only one dream this week. I want to remember my dreams.

ANALYST: I see you have written your dream in your book. That's a good sign, to write your dreams in a bound notebook and date each dream.

DREAMER: But I can hardly decipher the notes I scribbled in the middle of the night last Wednesday.

ANALYST: It is not enough to scribble your dreams in the middle of the night or even in the morning. You must rewrite them so you can decipher them. And when you do that, you will probably remember more details about the dreams.

DREAMER: I might be spending all my time writing dreams.

ANALYST: The first rule of the Dream Log is common sense. Just make it a significant aid to studying your dreams. Don't make it a career. If you are recalling a huge quantity of dreams, then use the rule of thumb. Like a garden, prune it.

DREAMER: Some people keep a flashlight by their bed and sit up and write the dream down very carefully as soon as they wake up with it. Some people use a portable tape recorder by the bed. I just like to scribble notes, but I will begin to rewrite them as you suggest.

ANALYST: How active are you when you wake up? I mean, do you bounce right up and rush around, or do you dally or just what?

DREAMER: I start rushing to get breakfast and go to work.

ANALYST: Then set your alarm clock fifteen minutes earlier, and take that extra time to work on your dreams.

DREAMER: What else?

ANALYST: The main thing is how you appreciate your dreams, I mean, how carefully you pay attention to them and think about them and look up in the reference books things that are strange but which you feel are important in your dream. You could draw them with stick figures and sketches of objects and use color if the dreams are colorful.

DREAMER: I think knowing I am coming here to tell you about my dreams is important because I remember my dreams more vividly the nights before I come here.

ANALYST: That is a reflection of you giving your dream life more value. The greater value you give it, the more it will reveal to you.

DREAMER: Maybe I *ought to pray* for a dream before I fall asleep.

ANALYST: "Oughts" are no good. Dreams on demand with the intercession of God is like passing the buck. Just keep it simple. Value your dreams and show your unconscious you are interested in it. It will speak more clearly to you.

DREAMER: You cite these short, clear dreams in your book. I have more complicated and obscure dreams.

ANALYST: Yes, but you also will have short, clear dreams. One of those is often enough. If you work on one dream, you will often find all you need to know at that time.

DREAMER: You sound like a dream salesman making a pitch.

ANALYST: I am making a pitch for people to remember and honor their dreams. We are all quite remarkably wise when we are asleep. You don't want to miss the best show in town, do you?

DREAMER: You exaggerate.

ANALYST: Maybe . . . but dreams are bigger than you think.

DREAMER: My best friend says just to forget dreams and live in the real world. She's a super-extravert and not really interested in this kind of thing.

ANALYST: Then dreams are not her cup of tea. But I'll bet that she has had or will have some dreams that really have a powerful effect on her. People shouldn't force themselves into the dream world.

DREAMER: Well, an introvert like me is more interested in the inner world. It is just natural for me to be introspective. And it wasn't until I read Jung that I realized that being introverted and valuing introspection is as normal as being extraverted and the good-old-American outgoing kid.

ANALYST: Well, pleasant dreams! Oops! I mean any old kind of dream for which we will be thankful. It would be nice to have a pleasant dream, though.

"Day 3,762: Still dead."

Drawing by Cheney; © 1989
The New Yorker Magazine, Inc.

EIGHT

Dreams: On Losing Your Head

Many years ago, I heard Yolanda Jacobi, one of Jung's famous analysands, lecture at the C. G. Jung Institute in Zurich. She was a cerebral person who wrote brilliant books about Jungian psychology. When she started her analysis, she said, she told Jung the dream she had before her appointment. She was walking out of Lake Zürich carrying a silver tray on which lay her head. Jung laughed and said, "Now, at last, you can begin your analysis." She explained in the lecture that Jung thought her unconscious was telling her that, first of all, she had to emerge from the waters of the unconscious without her head so she should be in touch with her feelings. Too much thinking. The brilliance of Jung's comment never left me.

Ask any old Jungian psychologist about the meaning of someone being headless in their dream and the odds are that they will give you some variant of the above idea. But it is not always so simple and never a cookbook interpretation.

"*It's got to come out, of course, but that doesn't address the deeper problem.*"

"Depth" Psychologist #1: Soul-making around the axis mundi constellates the archetypal shadow which always wounds in the unguarded back. In dealing with the sword of the trickster and the heart of the spiritual ecologist in the post-thinking state, one may understand the nekya while the gods and goddesses of our dreams meditate.

"Depth" Psychologist #2: In other words, "Ya gotta stop the hemorrhage first."

Drawing by Lorenz; © 1988
The New Yorker Magazine, Inc.

Can we not draw a lesson from history? If the practice of Jungian psychology continues the alchemical tradition, then we too—unless we are fully yellow—simply repeat its fate, falling prey to either physical scientism, spiritual esotericism, or the business of professionalism as princes in the world—or all three mixed. For our work to approach its cosmic purpose, for it to reach the world, it must spoil itself. "The withering away of the state" (Karl Marx). "Displacing the subject" by deconstructing its own consciousness (French philosopher Jacques Derrida). Self-destruct as damage control. Kill the Buddha. Apocalyptic via negativa. Catastrophe theory. Shevirath Ha-Kelim or Breaking the Vessels (Hillman 1991, p. 94).

HILLMAN

Furthermore, those analysands who turn on us, turn on analysis, who condemn, sue, expose, violate the trust, may actually be angels of the yellow road to the emerald city, angels in the salvation of the cosmos from the psyche closed long enough into individualism, sulfuric angels pointing the way at the end of this analytic century to an end of analysis that omits the world. . . . Nine months ago I ceased practicing private analysis. I continue to practice psychology with large groups, in public speaking and teaching, publishing and writing. These activities are permeated with the same sulfuric fumes that have characterized this paper and others corrosive to the white psychology which other parts of me have long championed. . . . I attribute this conviction to a predominance of sulfur in conjunction with mercury (Hillman 1991, p. 95).

HILLMan

Listener #1: What does that mean?

Listener #2: Like what it says, that analysands who turn on analysts and sue them are angels on the yellow road to the emerald city. So he retires from being an analyst.

Listener #1: Yes, but what is our cosmic purpose?

Listener #2: Sulfur in conjunction with mercury.

I worked for two years analyzing a Vietnam combat veteran who had been the point man leading seventeen men into an ambush where they were all killed. He alone escaped. When he returned the next day with other soldiers to recover the bodies, his men had all been decapitated, their heads stuck on punji sticks, and their faces smeared with feces. Soon thereafter, my patient became psychotic and was evacuated to the United States. Twelve years later, when he came to see me, he was tormented by a nightly recurring nightmare in which he relived his catastrophic trauma. When he began to recover, the nightmare changed. At first, he dreamed he was decapitated by the Vietcong, and he was running down a hill trying to grab his head before it rolled into the sea. I asked him how he could see without his head and he said he thought he could see with his soul, which came out of his neck. We worked with this dream experience off and on for months, rarely interpreting it, but listening to it in its many variations. He was living too much in his unconscious, not enough in his rational head. He was obsessed by feelings and memories and could not escape guilt and the deaths of his men. It was as if his head was still in Vietnam, as if his identity was inseparable from his buddies. He would wake from his dream screaming and drenched with sweat. Finally he dreamed that I was in the ravine, badly wounded in my head, and he rescued me. It was the first time he awoke crying and not terrified. He had rescued the *Wounded Healer,* myself, whom he saw carrying his suffering of Vietnam. He used his head to get me out of Vietnam, and so I could help him in the same way. The nightly recurrent dreams then gradually ceased.

To think it was good for the patient to lose his head in Vietnam, one would have to have a fixed attitude. He might have done better had he let it roll into the sea of the unconscious. That head should be left and buried in Vietnam so he could live in the here and now.

Another Vietnam combat veteran whom I analyzed had this recurrent dream:

> *I see blood pouring out of nowhere. I see the faces of my friends. Dead. I see battles and RPGs (rocket-propelled grenades) and tracers going off. I hear explosions and see flames of napalm. Dead, mutilated bodies, screams. I see a chaplain giving last rites to a head.*

The religious ritual focused on the head, all there was left of the soldier. The head, the soul. I cannot imagine the chaplain giving last rites to a hand or a foot. The head is the head of violent death cut off from life.

A classical Freudian analyst might see this image as castration, displaced upwards, symbolic of the universal male fear of castration by the father. A Freudian might see the Catholic priest as a symbol of the neurosis of religion and the *Father* would be relating to the son in death. The ubiquitous Oedipus.

There are endless ways to interpret the headless body, from fairy tales to losing one's head and being crazy, from blowing one's mind to mindless behavior, from punishment and one-sided headiness to the dismemberment of the heretic or the criminal shadow. Every once in a while, it might even relate to the Oedipus complex. And now and then, it might even be a joke.

Since this is a Jungian book, I might even refer to the *dead head* of alchemy: *caput mortuum,* a term to designate the residue left after exhaustive distillation or sublimation; hence, anything from which all that rendered it valuable has been taken away. In other words, not much of anything at all.

> Here here, ye symbols of the night.
> Here here, ye images of delight,
> of fright and flight.
> Any old meaning can be glued to
> any old image in any old dream, too.
> So how do we know the right light
> in which to see the dream?
> *Answer:* it all depends.
> *So,* a weasel answer!
> Not quite right:
> The answer is more the owl
> and the hawk of healing.

How a Recurrent and Unchanging Dream Finally Changes

After months or years of the same nightmare recurring with the images of a traumatic event, there is a sudden change. Instead of the scene viewed in various vivid realities, something new and unexpected enters the dream scenario. At first the change is something that did not actually happen, but could have possibly occurred. The replay tape has been altered.

The next element which alters the dream is an event that could not possibly have happened. The story takes a surreal twist, signaling the beginning of a connection with the present or an allegorical change. The psyche is processing the dream trauma until it takes the form of an ordinary nightmare with its hallucinatory images. The healing nightmare has evolved.

For eighteen years, the same nightmare plagued a Vietnam veteran. He awoke night after night in a sweat as if he was still in Vietnam.

He was very "tight" with his buddy, as the men called it, and they felt the love of comrades for each other. In a firefight, his buddy, standing beside him, was killed. Through the ghastly sight and total helplessness he realized that although it was his buddy who died, it might just as well have been him. His guilty conscience tore into him with the thought that he was glad he was alive and his buddy was dead, but bereft at the horrible death of his companion. The nightmares came:

> *My buddy has been shot. His body is like a bloody carcass. He is bleeding to death and I can do nothing. He is screaming. I yell, "Medic!" He is taken off by a Medivac helicopter still barely alive. I thought that once he had told me that he really loved me, but I had said nothing. And I kept saying to him, "You will be all right!" but not how much I cared for him. And when the bodies were taken off at the base, they lined them all up on the tarmac on stretchers. There are hundreds of bodies and I am watching them unload. When I see my buddy, he is dead. I wake up in a cold sweat, screaming.*

I began to see this veteran in psychotherapy and I listened. Each day he told me the same nightmare and how he could not get away from that memory and the feeling that he should have told him how deeply he loved him instead of lying to him by telling him he would be all right. The guilt about lying instead of telling the truth, about the impossibility of reconciling that feeling eighteen years later, plus the survivor guilt that unconsciously is "I'm glad it was you and not me," gnawed at his soul. I did not know what the dream meant, only that the dream process would probably unfold to tell us the meaning of the trauma. Then one day, about six months later, he told me that the dream had changed:

> *The same beginning of the dream but this time when I come to the stretcher on which had been his corpse, the stretcher is empty and I feel he is alive! And I go searching for him.*

Now my inner thoughts were: "At last. It is impossible to be reconciled with a dead body or to say what you obsess about not having said, and since, in the dream, his buddy is alive in a sort of resurrection, I can see what the search is about and that, in the world of dreams, he can say to his buddy what the dead body would not hear, what he failed to say to the dying buddy because he wanted to comfort him in his pain. So how do I formulate that to my patient? Like this . . .

WILMER: Now your buddy lives in the dream world, and you can tell him what you did not or could not say before. You can say it in a dream, or even in your imagination, because he still lives there. It would be a kind of spiritual experience because at last he is "all right."

VETERAN: It is almost as if he knew I was looking for him all those years and the power of my thoughts gave him life.

WILMER: Yes. Something like that. But don't count on a miraculous dream in which he appears and you two talk. It might happen, but more likely you will have different kinds of nightmares which you and I can interpret and finally this first repetitive dream will diminish and stop.

And that is what happened.

With the nightmares, like we all have (in which more personal day-by-day things appear and change in a kind of hallucinatory manner), it was possible to help him see how in his childhood there was a time when he also hadn't told someone he loved how much he cared, and the other person was killed in an accident. I do not want to give the impression that I talk about such things when I hear the catastrophic nightmare, or even that I search for childhood memories. If the patient brings up such associations, that is another matter, but almost always the horror of the unshakable dream like a monster preoccupies his mind. That preoccupation is what the therapist should keep in mind and not play at analysis because this has a subtle way of alienating a combat veteran and reducing him to a psychiatric case history when, in fact, he is living in an existential tragedy in which both symbol and metaphor are reduced to the most terrible thing he has ever seen. So let him or her have the nightmare, listen carefully, and do not trivialize anything. Approach it as if the psyche has some reason to do this and the dream has some meaning that you do not know. Being too smart and too clever can be actually a danger and can drive off the dreamer in disgust or feeling, "You were not there. You can't possibly know!" If we don't know the cause for the dream, accept that we don't know, and value the psyche. It has a way of leading us to answers.

Catastrophic post-traumatic nightmares are a unique form of dreams. There are no other dreams like them. Freud despaired of working with or considering them, because they were exceptions to his theory of dreams. They were not wish fulfillment, and they were not explainable in terms of libido theory. He did not treat any war neuroses. Jung, too, was pessimistic about treating them, saying that one had to wait and let the dreams more or less play out and stop of their own accord. However, in 1983 at Davos, Switzerland, I asked Marie-Louise von Franz, Jung's collaborator and one of the most illustrious Jungian authorities, why Jung didn't work with these combat nightmares. She told me that, in fact, he did and related this (unpublished) case.

A British officer came to Jung because of a war nightmare that had tormented him for several years after World War II. In the dream, the man is in his home and suddenly becomes terrified. It is night. He goes to the front door and locks it. Then the back door. He locks all the windows on the first floor. But the sense of terror and panic continues to build, and he goes upstairs and locks all the windows, but just as he begins to close the last window a grenade explodes outside the window. The dream recurs again and again during three months of analysis, until suddenly one night, when he goes to close the last window, a roaring lion appears and the dreamer wakes in terror.

Jung thought, "Ah, that's good. The instrument of danger has become an instinctual animal." And so it continues until finally, one night, as the dreamer closes the last window, he sees the face of a man. Jung said to himself, "Now he will not have the dreams anymore." And that was the case. The danger had been faced and was his own reflection, and that could be analyzed.

The Independent/*Michael Daley*

Drawn to illustrate an article about my experience with war dreams in which I referred to Jung's experience.

Reflections on the Dream Doorway

The door in the doorway must be opened carefully
and in its proper time.
At the threshold, consciousness and the unconscious meet.

There is a ritual to opening and closing doors,
to locking and unlocking doors.
Door comes from *duru* (OE), feminine.

I close my office door.
My room is an empty space
in which there are things and us.
It is a safe and limited space.
In case of dreaming,
please knock.

The doorway is an empty space,
in which we place a door.
But it is the essential opening
like the hub of the wheel.

> It is precisely where there is nothing
> that we find the usefulness of the wheel.
> We fire clay and make vessels:
> it is precisely where there is no substance
> that we find the usefulness of clay pots.
> We chisel out doors and windows:
> it is precisely in these empty spaces
> that we find the usefulness of the room.
> Therefore, we regard having something as beneficial;
> but having nothing as useful (Hendricks 1989, p. 63).

Dream as a Series of Doorways

Let us look closely at the dream as a symbolic presentation of the interface between the conscious and the unconscious psyche. In such a frame, it can be thought of as a doorway or many doorways. The dream then would be a threshold or gateway experience that can be looked at simultaneously as a passageway between two worlds.

Hermann Hesse, in his novel *Steppenwolf,* gives a fitting image:

> The wall was peaceful and serene and yet something was altered by it. I was amazed to see a small and pretty doorway with a Gothic arch in the middle of the wall, for I could not make up my mind whether this doorway had always been there or whether it had just been made. It looked old without a doubt, very old; apparently this closed portal with its door of blackened wood had opened hundreds of years ago into a sleepy convent yard, and did so still, even though the convent was not there. Probably I had seen it a hundred times and simply not noticed it. Perhaps it had been painted afresh and caught my eye for that reason. . . . I looked more closely. I saw over the portal a bright sign on which, it seemed to me, there was something written. I strained my eyes and at last succeeded in catching several words on end. They were:
>
> > "Magic Theater
> > Entrance not for Everybody" (Hesse 1963, pp. 33–34)

David (not his real name), a forty-year-old man, was deeply troubled by recurrent experiences in the night for twenty years. He said, "I am pursued by a misty gray cloud force or entity that seems like a *supernatural power.*" He had become increasingly depressed for a year.

David had never received any psychological help. Speaking of his experience, he said he did not know if this entity or force was good or bad, but it was a power that wanted to touch him. It had been getting closer in the weeks before he called me for an appointment. David was a man of modest means and held an ordinary job. He told me, apologetically, "I am really a simple person. I find it very hard to put my ideas into words."

His mother had died when he was only three days old, and sometime in the first few months of his life his father disappeared. He was left with his paternal grandparents whom he described as cruel and contemptuous so that he felt like a total outcast, unwanted and bereft following the mysterious circumstances of the disappearance of his mother and father. He described a perilous, traumatic childhood that he managed to survive. He sometimes abused other children as he had been abused.

His grandmother told him that his mother had fallen at home and suffered a head injury that caused her death. He was not so sure, and the mystery of his mother's death preyed on him. At seven, his father returned, and soon thereafter David persuaded his father to send for him and take him to his home. His stepmother was kind and caring.

After seeing me for four hour-long sessions, David told me his first dream. As it turned out, he reported only one more dream in fifteen months of therapy. He recalled no others. The first dream:

> I am in a large room like your office, with a row of three patio windows from floor to ceiling. Outside, I can see the woods just like from your office windows. I am standing at the foot of some steps by a door in the back of your office which leads to your home [there is no such door in my office]. I am watching what is happening in your office as if I am watching a movie, or I am a camera and the whole thing is being recorded.

> A little boy about seven years old is standing by the chair where I usually sit, by the patio window. His arms are outstretched above his head and his hands are on the window. Outside, I can see misty smoke like a dark cloud . . . the force that had been after me all these years.

> There is no one in the office but me and the little boy. Then, all of a sudden, the dark mist clears and a woman stands there all in white. I know she is my mother, but at the same time, I am not sure who she is. She walks to the window and reaches up with her hands to match the position of the little boy's hands, their fingers separated by the glass but touching like against a mirror. My mother had come for reassurance that I was in a safe environment. I know that she wants to come into the room, but I can feel she is in a different dimension. It was a wonderful experience because she radiated love and peace. There is a large glass patio door which now appears to the right side of the boy [There is no such door in my office]. It is an unlocked sliding door, but I know that I cannot open it. One cannot go outside because one would be in a different world. I wake up with a peaceful sense of security.

For a man who had great difficulty expressing himself in words, he had done remarkably well in describing his dream. The age of the little boy, of course, was the age when he saw his father for the first time since he had left when David was a few months old. The dream seemed to

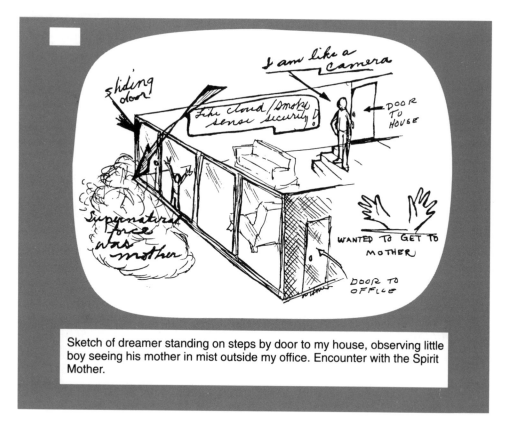

Sketch of dreamer standing on steps by door to my house, observing little boy seeing his mother in mist outside my office. Encounter with the Spirit Mother.

have the numinous quality of an archetypal vision. Of course, he had no real memory of his mother's face, so the uncertainty of recognizing the woman as his mother may have that reality basis, but the woman as mother could be the symbolic archetypal mother, the spirit mother . . . in the natural setting of the earth mother.

It was as if his mother had come back from the dead to see how he was doing and if he was safe and to reassure him of her eternal love and connection, that she, too, was trying for reunion. But she could not pass through the doorway to the land of the living nor could the little boy open the door to the land of the dead, although it was unlocked.

To have embraced his mother's specter would have meant a reunion in death. This, I suspected, was a force in his suicidal thoughts. I made a sketch of the dream.

I asked him what he thought the dream meant, and he reflected: "I was standing there watching the little boy touching the window, but I couldn't influence what was happening. I had no control over it. It was the same story—the entity was trying to touch me, but there was the glass. I understood that it just couldn't be done. In the dream, I just looked and accepted the fear I had been feeling."

"How could you do that?" I asked, as I wanted him to carry the feeling of how to master fear into consciousness.

"Because it was reality," he said, "and the being [mother] knew that I was being taken care of and no longer in a hostile environment. She was OK but in a different world, as I said. It *was* my mother [he said this as if convincing himself]."

I call this kind of dream the healing nightmare (Wilmer 1986) which I find is characteristic of the transformation of the post-traumatic nightmare. Usually it follows a long series of repetitive traumatic nightmares, but in David's case this was not so.

David's dream is uniquely complete in detail, construction, evolving drama, even to the sensation of being filmed by the dreamer as camera—a remarkable expression for the so-called "participant observer" (Wilmer 1968b). His suicidal ideas diminished after the dream and then stopped.

As his analysis was being terminated, one month before his last appointment, I remarked that he had told me only one dream, which I considered very important, and I reviewed it with him. I then asked him for permission to use it in this book. He readily agreed, and added, "There is something more that I want to tell you about that dream."

I reacted with rapt attention, because we had not talked about that dream for a year.

He said, "I don't know how to describe how serious the child [situation] is now. It is *any* child in danger. The dream told me the strength of the entity force and whether or not my mother would have wanted anything to harm her children."

This insight was a revelation to me on how the dream helped to overcome his fears. I had not thought of that. Then he told me an even more fascinating observation he had made and had never spoken of:

"When I first began talking with you, you would sometimes get sleepy, and I realized that you didn't know that the entity would be right around me at that time, and you couldn't see it, and I couldn't get you to see it." He had certainly become articulate. "It was happening in your office, and no one but I could see it because it was like a dark misty cloud. When I talked to you, it was as if you were asleep and couldn't see it." [I did recall being sleepy during some of these hours but he could barely put in words what he wanted to say. Now he was telling me that I had been unconscious of what he was experiencing, and I didn't know how true it was until this hour more than a year later.]

He went on:

"I had this entity, and I wanted to get your attention. I knew you weren't really asleep, but it was kind of a mixture of awake and asleep. I just couldn't get your attention so you could see what was all over me, closing in. It was terrifying."

I was astonished. He had never spoken to me of my sleepiness, but I had been painfully aware of it, and I had tried but could not figure out why I was sleepy unless it was that I was bored. David was a challenge to me. He was always eager to come to his sessions and could work with the transference. I puzzled over the countertransference and my sleepiness but couldn't figure it out. Why hadn't I brought this up with David, which is my usual approach to such a situation?

Then I was struck by a startling intuition. It was as if David's dark cloud was surrounding me, too, and I was rendered sleepy by the very force that was creating such terror and vigilance in him, you see, as if "the force" was putting me to sleep. Now I know this might sound like a cop-out for my inattentiveness, but I don't think so. Since the cloud was his projective image, I could not have seen it. It could project its force onto me by inhibiting him as if he were fading into the distance, like I was. One could put this in the imaginative fantasy of his being hostage to the cloud that threatened him by closing in on him if he were to cry for help. He did fear it was a lethal force. I am not talking about delusions and hallucination, because he never had any psychotic symptoms, and extensive psychometric tests ruled that out.

Two weeks before he terminated therapy, he told me a second dream that was a sort of epilogue to his other dream. How meager, yet how extraordinarily rich, his two dreams were.

> *I am in a room like your office with the same windows and sliding doors as the other dream. In fact, it is like the other dream except your office is longer. I am walking around the room and the dark cloud is around the woman* and *me. We walk together and I feel safe. Then she seems like my grandmother, then my stepmother. Then, with a final change, I had the feeling she was my natural mother.* Period! *The mother was a Mother Protector that came into your office. As we walked around—she was on my left side—the cloud was around us like an aura, but sometimes it would disperse and go away and that gave me a lot of confidence. Then I was startled to realize that it was* not me *with my mother, but my* seven-year-old little boy *walking around with his mother in that protective cloud. I could see it very clearly now because I was standing on the stairs [as in the first dream] watching it all happen. I woke up.*

David went on, "I now have a sense of security that I didn't know before. Instead of letting power crush you, you let the power work for you." As if to reassure *me,* he explained that while all of this might seem strange, it was "all right" and the only problem he had was "the difficulty I have in being able to be clear in explaining this to you." Little did he realize how eloquent his dreams and narrative had become.

Jung wrote: "And, just as a 'door' opens to one who 'knocks' on it, or a 'way' opens out to the wayfarer who seeks it, so, when you relate to your own (transcendental) centre, you initiate a process of conscious development which leads to oneness and wholeness. You no longer see yourself as an isolated point on the periphery, but as the One in the centre. Only subjective consciousness is isolated; when it relates to its centre it is integrated into wholeness . . . The paradoxical identity and difference of ego and self could hardly be formulated more trenchantly" (Jung 1954a, par. 427).

One Dream Is Enough

On many occasions when patients bemoan
that they remember *no* dreams
and are disappointed that they cannot deliver a dream
to their therapy hour,
or when they complain of *too many* dreams—
"We can't possibly go through all of them—
where should I begin?"
I say, *One dream is enough.*

That usually stops them.
Some are annoyed, as if I don't value
all their wonderful productions.
Some are bewildered: what kind of analyst is this?
Doesn't he know about dream series?
So, they promise to bring lots of dreams
if they have had a dream drought.
Still I say, *One dream is enough.*

This is impressive in the case where someone
has a vivid dramatic dream
with a profoundly providential message.
The patient may be willing to say,
One dream is enough.

But I do not mean it quite that way.
I mean that any symbolic dream narrative
remembered vividly is enough to work on
at any given time.
My theoretical idea is that
from any one such dream we can find
all we really need to know.
The one dream contains all the images of all dreams.
Even a part of one such dream is enough.

This idea allows one to accept the natural fate
of *all* dreamers who can neither remember all
of any one dream, or all of the dreams of any one night.
Occam's razor: *Entia non sunt multipicanda,* which means:
Entities are not to be multiplied.
This axiom says
that all unnecessary facts of constituents being analyzed

are to be eliminated.
William of Occam dissected every question
with a razor.* Now this applies to a dream dissected by
not only razor but laser.

An individual dream can be thought of
as a hologram.
If you illuminate a subject, such as a group of people,
by a laser light and make a photographic plate of it,
the plate will show only meaningless patterns of swirls.
But if you project laser light back through it,
you will see the people in three dimensions, and
you can project that image and walk among the people
seeing them from in front or behind.
But is it even more remarkable and mysterious
that if you cut the photographic plate in half
and then project the laser light,
the whole picture is seen.
No matter how tiny is the photographic plate's fragment,
the entire image is contained in it. Nothing is left out.

Research now is deeply involved in this process
in which the brain is seen as a hologram, and maybe
even the universe (Wilber 1982; articles by K. Pribram,
D. Bohm, and F. Capra).
Memory, communication, the art of psychotherapy,
and the wisdom of ancient religions and mystics
might be a part of science or vice versa.
The oneness of the universe may not be a metaphor
or expression of faith, but a fact.
Even such Buddhist ideas as "supreme identity"
and "all in one, one in all," and "what is above
is below" can be conceptualized as holographic paradigms,
and synchronicity, spirit, and the archetype of the Self,
even the art of psychotherapy and analysis
of dreams can be understood as an infinitesimal
fragment of a "photographic plate"
that can be illuminated by the laser light of
the mind.

---

*William of Occam, medieval scholastic philosopher, England, 1349. He taught that universal concepts were natural signs based on the similarity that we discover in things by experience. He denied the competence of reason in matters of faith, and said divine action was beyond any standards of human rationality.

So David's dream, one segment occurring at the first month
of analysis and the other fourteen months later,
might be just this sort of transcendental experience.
I am *not* implying that I hope my patients will
tell me or recall only one dream;
on the contrary, it is extraordinarily important to
remember and *write down* all the dreams you can,
but the purpose is like in mining;
there will come one gem, and that should be enough.
What I am telling my patients when I say
"One dream is enough"
is that any single, clear, symbolic dream is a great gift.

> Heaven above
> Heaven below
> Stars above
> Stars below
> All that is above
> Also is below
> Grasp this
> And rejoice
>
> *Theoria Athanasius Kircher,*
> *alchemist*

I am going to tell you about a way that I use
with small groups to study how to
understand and interpret a dream. There
are four basic ideas: 1) Follow the dream
line or story. 2) Number the sequences 1, 2,
3, etc. 3) Carefully note and record all
words spoken or appearing in the dream. 4)
Note the metaphors in the story, dialogue,
and images. Do not, repeat, do not interpret
a dream until you have first understood the
images of the manifest dream, and then the
dreamer's associations before the
interpretation. *NOW READ THE TEXT.*

Jungian Dream Group

Experiential Group Method for Learning a Discipline

I have employed the following method to teach my Jungian approach to dream analysis to a wide variety of people. For many years, I used it with psychiatric residents, psychology students, psychiatrists, general public groups, as well as schizophrenic veterans and Vietnam combat veterans with post-traumatic stress disorder. While a group of eight to ten people is the preferable size, it can be carried out effectively with groups of up to twenty. Managing a dream group with larger numbers requires a high degree of social psychological skill as well as unique sensitivity and appreciation of the dramatic tendencies in participants and leaders of large groups. It demands a sense of active leadership and a capacity to facilitate a wide but limited time contribution from participants. As in all group process, if the leader does not lead and lacks the facility to keep individuals from domineering in the group and forcing cliques, it can be just controlled chaos.

Some dream group analysts, such as Montague Ullman, have created a unique technique without the leader role I have described. In these groups each dream shared is discussed as if it is the dream of each group member (Ullman 1988, pp. 1–26).

With common sense, clinical experience, and some degree of wisdom and empathy, an experiential Jungian dream group can be an extremely enlightening experience. I find an easel with a large pad of white paper and a well-inked, black felt-tip pen most valuable. I draw the dream, using stick figures and rough sketches, lines to show sequence and arrows to emphasize. This is valuable in training people to listen and remember. By objectifying the spoken story into minimal simple images, everyone can experience the process of memory modeling and image encoding. It also keeps the leader at a high pitch of attentiveness.

OK, Dr. Wilmer. I'm following you, but I am also getting lost in a lot of ideas. Maybe you'd better tell me how it is done in action. Otherwise, I think I'll take the Grayline tour.

Sorry about that.

OK. For example, twenty people have signed up for a dream workshop called "Experiential Dream Group. Be prepared to bring your own dream." After the introductions and some simple comments about what I have just told you, I explain the steps and the exact order in which we will follow them.

Now I'm with you. So, who tells a dream? There are twenty people?

I say, "Will anyone who has a dream to tell the group please write your name on a piece of paper and pass it to me. I would prefer that it be a short dream, and it would be best if it was recent, like this morning. But any short recent dream will do. Then I will put the names in a sack and have someone draw out the name of the person who will tell us a dream. After the dream is told, I will pull another name from a sack that includes the entire list of participants. That person will retell the dream as nearly verbatim as possible. Since you do not know who that person will be, you must each be ready for it to be you."

After the dream has been told, the dreamer is asked to tell briefly what was happening at the time of the dream that might have influenced it.

What if no one has a dream? What if someone says it is short but it is really long and complicated? What if someone tells you a dream so crazy that you would feel uncomfortable having the dream group work with it?

Good questions. I am sorry that I didn't tell you that *before* I hear the dream, I say I reserve the privilege to decide whether I think it is appropriate for this kind of dream group. If for any reason I decide it is not, I will draw another name from the sack. Usually I can tell within a few minutes whether it would be unwise to deal with the dream in this kind of group. It rarely happens, but it might. No one seems to mind except the dreamer, and you must present it in such a way that everyone seems to understand. With this candor and flexibility, you build a feeling of group trust and a necessary commitment to your leadership. I haven't encountered a group without a dream in many years.

I think a group "leader" should be a "facilitator," not a true leader! You sound like a commandant.

Maybe to you. Facilitators work for other kinds of groups. I do not say "take my word for it." As commandant, I simply establish rules and rituals for the process so it can help and not hurt anyone. You can process one or two dreams in a half-day session with a coffee break in the middle. If the leader is genuinely empathetic, sensitive, and informed rather than autocratic, full of hubris, or condescending, then it will work out quite well *because the group will have a healing power and a helping atmosphere.*

Oh? What happens after the dreamer has told a dream and a group member has retold the story?

I tell the group at the start that while they can take notes as the dream is related, since I will be writing on the pad, they *cannot use any notes* in retelling the dream and I will turn over the pad or cover the blackboard. If you don't say this at the beginning, you will have the dreary experience of listening to someone read notes they have scribbled, and you will have failed to teach anyone to rely on their ears first and foremost. The notes or sketches jog the memory, but telling someone a dream without referring to a single note is a very special experience.

One of the most important things a therapist or group can do is retell the dream to the dreamer, for in so doing, everyone hears it, realizing that it has been processed in another person's mind.

That seems pretty cool to me. I think that's good. But what if the person retelling didn't tell it right?

They hardly ever do. That is the point! If you listen to a dream and then talk to the dreamer without giving the dreamer a chance to be sure you heard it right, you can be talking about two different dreams. Well, that is the value of the group because next you ask the group to add to the details of the dream retold or correct any errors in fact, metaphor, sequence, or whatever.

Now at least everyone in the group has the same dream story in mind. Meanwhile, the leader will correct on the sketch pad any mistake or omission he has made. Everything is almost ready for the next step. I always make one admonition, however. I call it "The O.B.T.W.," or the "Oh, by the way. . . ." You can be quite certain that the dreamer will often recall some element of the dream after it has been told. This aspect might come to mind immediately after telling the dream or in hearing it retold or even later. You can be pretty sure that the "Oh, by the way . . ." is the clue to the dream. It has been momentarily repressed and then brought back to memory. If you can tell what jogged the dreamer's memory, that might be quite helpful, but just the experience itself will be enlightening and add to the zest of the process.

Could you give me an outline for the various stages through which you will lead the group? After the dream is told and retold, then what can we expect?

(1) Each image is discussed and the relationship of objects to each other and the entire setting is explored. The group is strictly held to the "manifest content of the dream" and not permitted to leave its details. This is a kind of sensation, a factual inventory of the elements within the dream sequences.

(2) Members describe their feelings on hearing the dream and ask the dreamer for feelings experienced in the dream. Note the dreamer's feeling reactions to what is said in group. The dream may be divided into sequences, maybe two to four parts, as few divisions as possible (like acts in a play). These are numbered on the sketch. Spoken words are carefully written on the sketch because all words either spoken or seen in a dream are potentially of great significance. You may explore the dream ideas as story or not story but cannot make any interpretation yet.

(3) The dream metaphors, symbols, and bizarre, illogical parts are explored for their unconscious meanings, and the group and dreamer may fantasize about the images and the story. . . . Then the dreamer is asked to give an interpretation: what he or she thought it meant when he first recalled it, and what he thinks it means now that he has had the dream group experience. After that, each member in turn, going around the circle, is asked to give a very short interpretation—no lectures, no long explanations, just what it means. The leader summarizes and brings the interpretations into one coherent brief idea using and acknowledging key thoughts of group members. The dreamer is given the last word: "Any comments?" Then it is finished. The leader does not permit anyone in the group, himself or herself included, to speak after the dreamer's final statement. Often someone can not bear not to have the last word. That is where the commandant steps in.

Final Rules of Thumb

(A) Sit in a circle if possible. If there are twenty to thirty members in the group, I suggest that you sit in two concentric circles. The inner circle will work with the first dream, while the members of the outer circle are prohibited from speaking. It works! They are the audience. They may also be rehearsing in their minds. After a coffee break, the two circles change places so that the outer circle becomes the inner circle and processes the dream of one of its members. The outer circle remains silent.

(B) With larger audiences, improvise techniques for random audience participation. For example, you might limit the participation in each sequence of the process to members whose birthdays are in certain months, or whose last names begin with certain letters. You may divide the audience according to the special arrangement of the seating. It doesn't matter so much how you do it as long as everyone accepts the necessary management of the group.

(C) Keep a clear sense of time! Budget it so that there are fairly equal portions of time for each group task. Cut participation short when it is getting long winded. Do not hesitate to orchestrate. Remember that dream narration is often a conscious construct.

(D) Pay attention to anything anyone says. Do not ridicule. Never belittle anything anyone says, provided it is not in itself ridiculing and demeaning. If you give due respect to each thing that is said, you will find your audience respecting what you say and your guidance. Remember that whatever anyone suggests in a group, it is based on their truth. Don't be pompous. Be natural even if you have to fake it— by that, I mean have a decent persona, please.

Why do you go to all this trouble to present a technique when you warn against techniques?

First, you must have techniques before you can discard them. If you don't learn a discipline and an orderly, logical approach, you are not then free to move to the irrational realms of the soul.

Aphorisms

People without disciplined minds tend to act by the seat of their pants, claiming their unique privilege like the First Amendment's Freedom of Speech, to denounce freedom of speech.

Remember that a dream is not to be taken literally.
Remember that good answers do not come from "yes and no" questions.
Remember that any dream group will be shadow as well as light.
Remember the white chameleon dream, where the dreamer was taking a shower in a white stall and just happened to notice a pure white chameleon on the white tile.

Interpretations: All white and no shadow is a cause for alarm.

"Oh, by the way, there was a fragment of the dream that I forgot to tell you. All I remember is that someone gave me a piece of licorice to eat."

How can I keep all that stuff in my mind?

You can't.
Go join a dream group and see how it works.

NINE

When one is "posessed by an archetype," it is like being in the clutches of a darkness (shadow) which we might try to destroy, but this cannot happen in life or in dreams: the shadow always returns.

The Shadow: Themes and Variations

The shadow represents the personal unconscious that Freud discovered and an archetype of the collective unconscious that Jung discovered. A balanced Jungian psychology pays attention to the repressed life of childhood and later life experiences as well as the psyche, which is transpersonal—beyond our personal life experiences. This collective psyche is probably genetically transmitted—that is, we are born with a psyche prepared for our instinctual psychological life. It is not a *tabula rasa*.

An example of the collective shadow that we can easily recognize is the *bête noire* (black beast) that we project onto some individual whom we particularly dislike or detest. Each of us has a few such people. Some people are fixed on just one individual, and others have a stable full of such people, places, and races where we park our own shadow. Because of the racial (*bête noire*) significance of "black," we can equally speak of the "blond beast," which Jung called the animal instinct that takes over in Dionysian frenzy, seizing the "unsuspecting soul with nameless shudderings" so that one becomes hero and superhuman entity beyond good and evil. This is "identification with the shadow" (Jung 1943, pars. 40–41).

> The power of this archetypal takeover
> is so strong that it obsesses one
> and drains away energy from vital life tasks.
> It is as if we say to ourselves,
> "So that's the shadow! I can see who the villain is.
> It is this one. If it wasn't for him (or her),
> all would be OK."

> How cleverly that absolves us from any responsibility.
> Finally recognizing that "it" is this person,
> we don't have to feel any guilt or wrong in us.
> Once I decided to use some "active imagination"
> to sketch a picture of "him."
> This is what he looked like inside:
> Things swirling, hands reaching, tentacle arms moving,
> eyes everywhere casting distrust and suspicion,
> flickering tails, monster eyes searching,
> interlacing meshes and serrated cutting surfaces.
> It is a faceless specter,
> a helter-skelter force of mean energy.
> I had drawn a picture of my bête noire for my
> Rogues Gallery of Shadows I Have Known.

Now I could befriend my shadow,
and he could make me see a thing or two about myself
where I had been blind.

Now I could see the other previously threatening person
as an ordinary, not significant, opinionated oaf,

but not evil or inherently bad since he and I
were shadows of the other.

Gradually I could see that it was precisely where
he riled me most that I had to look most closely
and do something positive.
The *bête noire* thus becomes
a "psychic sonar" alerting me to dangers,
shoals and how to steer my course.

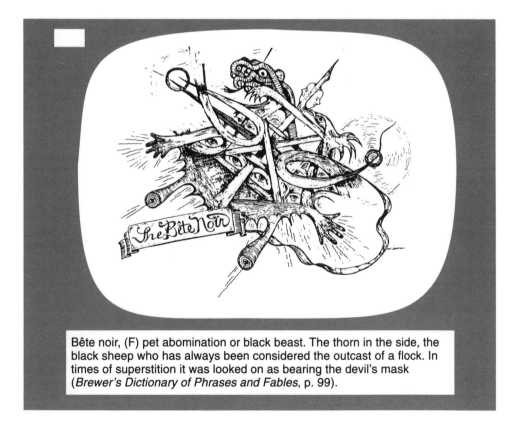

Bête noir, (F) pet abomination or black beast. The thorn in the side, the black sheep who has always been considered the outcast of a flock. In times of superstition it was looked on as bearing the devil's mask (*Brewer's Dictionary of Phrases and Fables*, p. 99).

Facing Your Shadow

If you can bring your unconscious conflicts into consciousness, will you have insight?

> No. It's not that simple.
> But you can then see the shadow,
> which was previously unconscious
> and only known in projections onto others
> of the unwanted, rejected parts of yourself
> that you despised or want to deny or hide or ignore.
> It is also part of our primitive animal nature.
> The shadow itself is neither bad nor evil.
> It is the negative hidden aspect of your psyche.
> There is both a personal
> and a collective (archetypal) shadow.

How do I get insight then?

> By facing your shadow,
> eating your shadow and digesting it,
> befriending your shadow,
> not running from your shadow.
> That's the beginning.

Where do I find these things you call shadow?

> In your dreams,
> they will appear as shady characters, criminals,
> all sorts of dangerous, unsavory things and events.
> The shadow figure, said Jung, is always
> of the same sex as the dreamer.
> You will find your shadow when you are awake
> in other people and things that offer hooks
> on which you can hang your shadow stuff.
> You will recognize it out there.

OK. Gotcha. So, I see this ugly, rejected side of myself in my dreams and in the people I can't stand. What is it, a kind of David and Goliath encounter?

> You know who won that one.
> Let me give you an example of a shadow dream:
> You are being pursued by an ominous force
> or a threatening beast, object, or person.
> You run from it.
> It keeps after you.
> But almost always,
> when you finally turn to face it,
> it will back down.

It will lose its ominous power.

> It is natural to try to avoid danger and pain,
> but it is often a tragic mistake to run,
> to "get the hell out of there,"
> to try to change life by changing wives, lovers, jobs, husbands,
> or to seek the surcease by drinking, drugs, affairs,
> and having children to cement cracked marriages.

I know lots of situations with people, places, and jobs where the better part of wisdom and valor would dictate getting out and finding someone or something more compatible.

> Yes, but the solution is
> not to run away or leave abruptly
> in anger, rage, or blame, spewing and castigating others
> and proclaiming your innocence.
> I'm not advocating giving up.
> I'm advocating a new kind of courage.
> When you run from the shadow,
> you increase its power over you.
> It is a bully that can grow into a monster.
> It thrives on intimidation,
> and yet it shrivels
> when you face it eyeball to eyeball
> and don't blink.

Well, I'm glad to hear that when you face the shadow and . . . what did you say . . . digest it, it disappears.

> I did *not* say it disappears.
> I said its power is diminished and it shrivels.
> Its peril evaporates from the scene,
> but it is essential to realize
> that the shadow never disappears.
> It always lurks in the unconscious's crevices.
> Once you make its acquaintance,
> you can remember ways to cope—
> maybe slowly
> or fast like a balloon that shrinks away
> when the air leaks out.
>
> It is said that only the devil has no shadow.
> The task is how to manage your own shadow.
> When you can do that,
> the shadow becomes an ally,
> rooting around in the dark places
> and letting you know by signals, symptoms, dreams, and anger
> where your own unconscious is brewing noxious things.

There you go again: "Brewing noxious things." Sounds like a witch.

> Yes, I know.
>
> A patient of mine dreamed that she was pursued
> by a huge, black, menacing force
> that was trying to kill her.
> For about three months,
> in a series of cliff-hanging dreams,
> she just managed to escape.
> Then the next installment came at her with incredible
> violence, gore, and terror.
> Her hiding places gave out,
> and she was running across a long, very narrow bridge
> on each side of which was the ocean.
> There were no railings,
> and as she ran, she saw behind her
> a huge, black, amorphous object gaining on her.
> Ahead was a beautiful home at the end of the bridge.
> The huge, black object was now so close
> she could see it clearly.

It was an insect, a bug about twenty feet high.
Suddenly, she stood stock still.
The blackness came at her,
but just before it reached her, it flew
up into the sky and sailed over the house.
When it hit, there was a great explosion.
The pieces of the bug flew out into the ocean.
She walked on to the house in great relief.
Parked by the back door where the object had hit
was an old-fashioned yellow Volkswagen "Beetle"
(what used to be called "the bug").
Quite a sense of humor in the old psyche.
You could almost call it an alchemical transformation.

Just like a Jungian. Slipping in the old alchemical curve when the mystery heats up. A yellow bug is not gold. I suppose you're going to say something about the soul and gold.

Why not?
Now that you mention it:
The most important alchemists were not
concerned with the manufacture of "common gold,"
of "*aurum vulgi*," but with the "*aurum nostrum*,"
the symbol of an illuminated soul (Jung 1975, p. 20).

The positive creative unconscious sounds like Pollyanna Milquetoast. What about the nasty part, that evil and foul side of humankind?

Yes. There is a deep, demonic unconscious,
the black quicksand into which we sink.
It is the power that drives addiction.
It is the love of money.
It is the Dark Castle of Hatred and Evil.
It is our criminal underworld
and our darkest melancholy,
the shattered Ten Commandments,
and the dung heaped on the gravestone
of the Golden Rule.

It is the dungeon of the furies and the voices
that cry out, "Kill him!" "Kill her!" "Kill anything!"
It is the Megapower of Compulsion and Obsession.
It is not only *not* friendly,
it is the abode of the Prince of Darkness
and the vile and infamous side
of everything good, virtuous, and divine.

Viewed psychologically,
it is our inherent inhumanity we must contain and conquer,
the very conquest by which we earn our humanity.

Taken symbolically,
it is myth and legend,
terrorism, torture, and the holocaust in our mind.
It is that part of our psyche that must die
so that our spirit can be reborn.
It is hell.

It is the flame of self-defeat and self-destruction,
of bigotry and prejudice incarnate,
anathema to love and caring.
It is the archetype of War.
It is the battlefield of humanity.
It is the crucible of character.

The Positive Shadow

It may be an unpleasant reminder to be kinder
to your shadow, which is going to be with you
all your life.
Treated well, it can knock your affectation
right off its pedestal.

The shadow is a helpful enemy; it has been called
our best enemy.
It reveals weaknesses by
getting under our skin and glowing and showing
where we are thin-skinned. With it,
you can see right through you.

Many living rituals in our Western culture
dramatize the shadow side of life
so as to gain power over it and belittle it.

It has been a carnival ritual in Zug, Switzerland,
since 1884 to have the procession of Greth-Schnell
and her companions, the "Loli" in which Greth-Schnell
carried her little, drunk man home in a basket
on her back under the derision of the population.

Such carnivals are collective expiations
as well as celebrations of darkness and light
to get things out of our systems.
For some such carnivals, it is evil and death
that are warded off.
It is the embodiment of the hidden side
of ordinary people who wear outrageous disguises
as if it isn't really us doing it at all.

In older cultures than ours, such rituals,
ceremonials, and archetypal reenactments
are far richer, less stylized,
and more spontaneously visceral.
We are always at war with these mythic powers
that can still save us, for they are more powerful
than our technology; they are like
the sun and heavens themselves,
which naked wear no clothes.

Carnival in Zug, Switzerland

DO NOT POINT

He did it.

She did it.

They did it.

Who me? I didn't do anything.

If we can only get him/her/it/them, we are going to be OK.

Blame someone else. Always. Always. Naturally.

Black and White. Red and Green.

or BLUE YELLOW.

A sure way to put your finger on the culprit.

The finger pointers of the world can never unite.

Jung cited a letter from a former patient who described
"the necessary transformation" in simple but trenchant words:

Out of evil, much good has come to me. By keeping quiet,
repressing nothing, remaining attentive, and by accepting
reality —taking things as they are, and not as I wanted them to
be—by doing all this, unusual knowledge has come to me,
and unusual powers as well, such as I could never have
imagined before. I always thought that when we accepted
things they overpowered us in some way or other. This turns
out not to be true at all, and it is only by accepting them that
one can assume an attitude towards them. So now I intend to
play the game of life, being receptive to whatever comes to
me, good and bad, sun and shadow forever alternating, and,
in this way, also accepting my own nature with its positive and
negative sides. Thus everything becomes more alive to me.
What a fool I was! How I tried to force everything to go
according to the way I thought it ought to!

(Jung 1957, par. 70)

JUNG

You say befriend your shadow,
that ugly part of yourself
in your unconscious.
Sounds fiendish.
What did Jung say about that?

Acceptance of oneself is the essence of the moral problem and the acid test of one's whole outlook on life. That I feed the beggar, that I forgive an insult, that I love my enemy in the name of Christ—all these are undoubtedly great virtues. What I do unto the least of my brethren, that I do unto Christ. But what if I should discover that the least amongst them all, the poorest of all beggars, the most impudent of all offenders, yea, the very fiend himself—that these are within me, and that I myself stand in need of the alms of my own kindness, that I myself am the enemy who must be loved—what then? Then, as a rule, the whole truth of Christianity is reversed: there then is no more talk of love and long-suffering; we say to the brother within us "Raca," and condemn and rage against ourselves. We hide him from the world, we deny ever having met this least among the lowly in ourselves, and had it been God himself who drew near to us in this despicable form, we should have denied him a thousand times before a single cock had crowed.

(Jung 1932, par. 520)

JUNG

Lessons from the Shadow

I returned from a trip to Switzerland earlier in the year, feeling jubilant, rested, and rather pleased with what I had accomplished and exhilarated by climbing some of the alpine paths on the Matterhorn. High above the mundane world, in the great silence and wonder of the world, I had the following dream:

> *I am talking with the High Commissioner of the United Nations in Geneva, Switzerland, who tells me that he wants me to meet a great Turkish chemist who would be a good speaker for me to invite to Salado, Texas. The scene changes and I am now in Salado, rushing to get to a noon conference. I am late. When I arrive this famous chemist is on the podium speaking. I realize that the High Commissioner had sent him to Salado without even notifying me. I walk up and interrupt him in order to introduce him. It is ridiculous because I realize I don't know anything about him, not even his name. So I fudge and mumble a name, then turn to him asking, "How do you pronounce your name?" He replies, "My name is pronounced Koko." I continue trying to cover up my ignorance by asking him insipid questions, but no one seems to pay attention to me or what I am saying. I wake up.*

Let me tell you a few associations to parts of the dream. I recently had a cordial meeting with the Deputy High Commissioner for Refugees at the UN in Geneva about a program on African refugees for the Institute for the Humanities in Salado, Texas. Who was the Turkish chemist? When I was in the Navy, stationed in Bethseda, Maryland, at the National Naval Medical Research Institute, the United States Surgeon General called to tell me that the Surgeon General of the Turkish Navy was coming to see me at noon. I became so flustered that I completely forgot the meeting. It was a matter of much embarrassment. These memories and the good news in my personal life fashioned the drama of my dream, which would teach me a lesson.

So who was Koko? I racked my brains. Cocoa made no sense to me. The cocoa beans which the natives of West Africa eat did not mean much, nor did the Swiss cuckoo clock. Then, as I pondered on the dream I suddenly remembered the words, "I am Koko, the Lord High Executioner" from Gilbert and Sullivan's operetta, *The Mikado.* In the operetta, which takes place in the tiny village of Titipu, the emperor is told that his son Nanki-Poo had been beheaded. In reality, it never happened because Koko never executed anybody. He was just a clowning pompous singer.

Now I understood the dream. I, like others, am sometimes carried away with the wonderful charm of Salado and the impressive speakers who visit the Institute for the Humanities there. We must all be able to accept the human comedy and our vulnerabilities.

Citizens of Titipu: This is Koko speaking.

The Shadow of the Therapist

In "The Case of Dr. Renee Richards," psychoanalyst Victor Bloom writes that Raskind had achieved considerable success as an ophthalmologist, but was a man troubled by fantasies of being a woman and was plagued by the desire to cross-dress as a woman. "He underwent years of psychoanalysis with some of the most highly recommended analysts, including Robert C. Bak, one-time president of the American Psychoanalytic Association. . . . The later part of his analysis with Bak deteriorated into the extensive use of direction, suggestions, and threats of impending psychosis if the patient 'acted out' to 'solve' his/her problem concretely—that is, by surgery. There was little indication of any empathic understanding on the part of his world-famous psychoanalyst; rather, Richards was implored to grow a beard, date women, get married, have a son, work as a doctor—in other words, conform to social expectations. . . . Like his mother, Richards's analyst was dominating, controlling, and relentless. The transference–countertransference impasse that resulted precluded the necessary empathy, and Richards had to flee the treatment and seek transsexual surgery."

The author of the article goes on to say: "This case has implications for us as psychoanalysts because of the current discourse about the relative influence of early intrafamilial psychosexual vs. later extrafamilial social factors in gender identity."

Just when the author had made explicit his point about the danger of dominating authoritarianism, of telling patients what they must do, of demanding it with threats of consequences if the advice is not taken, of the disaster of exploitation of the power of the analysts, of imposing his own values, and the overriding need for empathy, he lapses into as much nonsense about its implications as did the world-famous analyst. The implications he tells us are lost in the shrubbery of jargon.

I wish to cite the case of an analysand of a well-known Jungian analyst. This young woman was referred to the analyst because of confusion, identity conflict, and an inability to develop positive enduring relationships with men. She had become depressed. Given this kind of life crisis, almost everything depends on who is there "giving" the help. In her case she had made an unfortunate decision to stick with the analyst to whom she was referred despite her growing ambivalence and hatred. He unconsciously fulfilled her father image in reality and in fantasy. Thus, she was headed for a repetition of the very conflict that made her seek professional help in the first place.

Even though he was a Jungian analyst he told her (doctor's orders) authoritatively to lie down on his couch and he would analyze her. Note, "he would analyze her," a small misrepresentation of what analysis is really about. He might help her to analyze herself, or "in her analysis." Just words? Not so. In this case it was her submissive undoing. He insisted that his interpretations were right when she would question them, and now and then would say, "Just think about what I said. You will see" (doctor knows best).

On one such an occasion, after leaving his office and driving home in a blinding rainstorm, she panicked. Fearing that she was going to kill herself by yielding to the strong impulse to drive off the road, she stopped at a pay phone and called her analyst. She told him what was happening and he replied that "If you feel that way, you'll have to kill yourself." Then, he hung up.

This, no doubt, was intended to make her face the crisis in her struggle between living and dying. At that moment, she felt that she could never trust or depend upon him. She told him so at the next therapy hour. He replied that the goal of analysis was individuation. She must rely upon herself, not him or something out there. She must not rely on trusting "the father" to save her.

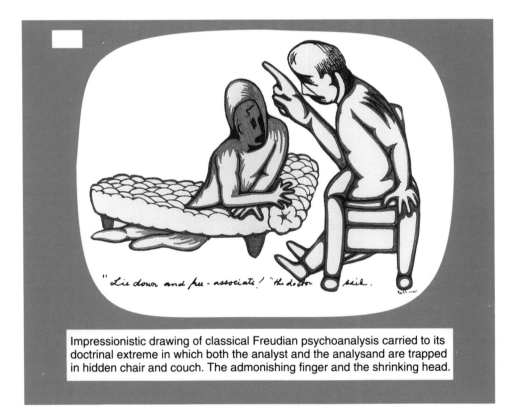

Impressionistic drawing of classical Freudian psychoanalysis carried to its doctrinal extreme in which both the analyst and the analysand are trapped in hidden chair and couch. The admonishing finger and the shrinking head.

The analyst interpreted this moment of therapy as the alchemical conflict between the spiritual quest and the manipulative quest of her shadow. Understood in such archetypal terms, he said she would see that this was not a personal transference to him but a transpersonal transference. In other words, he was hiding behind jargon and denying the human relationship that exists between analyst and patient.

Following this she began to feel she was crazy, that he was not the caring persona he assumed, but some kind of monster who was out to destroy her and her only salvation lay in not antagonizing him since she was "in his power." She told herself that maybe he was right, and that she ought to try to accept him and not tell him what was really on her mind or cry for help, because if she did he would hang up on her.

In the end she got the courage to leave him and found a Jungian analyst who could help her find her way to be free of depression. She had faced both her shadow and her analyst's shadow and they both lost their hold on her.

The Good Doctor's Shadow

On September 10, 1990, readers of *Newsweek* magazine were astonished to read a feature, "The Mind," with a large banner headline: "Beno Brutalheim? A Revered Child Psychologist Comes Under Attack for Abusive Methods."

Bruno Bettelheim, who committed suicide in March 1989 at the age of eighty-six, a survivor of Nazi concentration camps, was eulogized as one of the great psychoanalysts and thinkers of the twentieth century. He retained his humanity and devoted his life to treating the most emotionally disturbed children. A former patient, who had spent ten years at Bettelheim's Orthogenic School at the University of Chicago, wrote an article in the *Washington Post* accusing Dr. Bettelheim of a reign of terror, bullying, publicly humiliating, and physically abusing disturbed children in his care. Interviews with other patients, teachers, and counselors who had been at the Orthogenic School revealed abuses. *Newsweek* reported some of these events and the astonishing fact that his colleagues, his successor, counselors, analytic friends, and his own writings did not publicly mention the situation at his school. Bettelheim's friend, analyst Rudolf Ekstein was quoted as saying, "He had seen a dictator who destroys people, and he became a dictator who wanted to rescue people." The *Newsweek* article stated, "Chicago analysts now scathingly referred to the doctor as 'Beno Brutalheim.'"

Why were the patients silent? One of them said, "Who would believe us?" Although physical punishment was allowed when Bettelheim ran the school, it is now banned. Bettelheim had written, "Unfortunately, punishment teaches a child that those who have power can use force to do their will." This is the story of the shadow trickster who is one pole of the archetype of the hero and savior. At one extreme is terror, at the other saintliness. But should we think about the silent collusion of the shadow of professional colleagues? Would we have believed them? Would it have made any difference? Did the good outweigh the bad? Did the encounter with evil in the Nazi concentration camp evoke a dark power in Bettelheim that ultimately led to his depression and suicide? The value of the story is to see the shadow as teacher, that denial of the shadow, refusing to face it in conscious reality, also is an act of the trickster.

We all have a shadow. The larger the personality, the greater the shadow. The more the public persona is elevated, the more treacherous is the inner darkness. The point is to acknowledge this side and welcome having the light on our shadow.

Jung was painfully aware of his shadow and wrote much about it. He even kept a bust of Voltaire in his waiting room to remind his patients and himself that he did not want the patient nor himself to be deceived by the genial doctor.

THE THREE FACES OF THE SHADOW

PERSONAL — Repressed fantasies, wishes, impulses, and ideas etc. from personal life

COLLECTIVE — Power, greed, hatred and lust of an epoch, not individual in origin

ARCHETYPAL — Evil and absolute evil, demonic, the gods and the goddesses, mythology and prehistoric

PART

TEN

TRANSFERENCE

Projection: Transference/Countertransference

The feelings that you have about another person
may have their origins primarily in you—a matter of projection.
The most obvious example is the instantaneous hatred or love
that arises upon seeing or being with someone the first time.

Strong feelings about another person may surface only
when you perceive some aspect of their behavior or personality
that either warrants your reaction *or*
is simply a hook onto which you can easily hang your projection.
Your feelings and judgment seem reasonable and rational,
but don't kid yourself.
Remember that your reaction may be a response
to their projection onto you.

Remember that projections, your own or mutual,
are based on *unconscious* perception or apperception.
When the transference is positive, you are attracted,
and when it is negative, you are repelled.
Negative (or shadow projections) are the psychic explanation
of prejudice.

Love is a natural projection, which, Jung said,
is a mixture of personal and archetypal forces.
Its great power lies in the archetype that transcends
ordinary reality: It is the basis of the *complex*
into which lovers fall. It's the same for hatred.

The transference that occurs in analysis or psychotherapy
is both normal and intensified
by the process, rituals, and techniques.
It is one of the most important
and valuable experiences of therapy—
provided it is made *conscious and understood.*
Since the same process occurs in analysts
as *counter*transference, it behooves the therapist
to be fully conscious of countertransference.
This awareness is possible only if the therapist
has had personal analysis or psychotherapy.

Transference blooms
in the intimacy or closeness of analysis.
It becomes a tool with which the patient can understand
a basic factor in human relationships.
The fire in the relationship between analyst and patient
can get hot with anger, hatred, or
all sorts of thoughts and feelings
that are brewed in the unconscious
and bear little objectivity.

The source of transference
was originally thought to be infantile and childhood relations
to parents and parental surrogates.
Jung added that transference can be based
on archetypal complexes having nothing whatsoever
to do with one's subjective life.

The feelings and thoughts were said to be transferred
from the past to the present situation.
But transference is by no means so limited.

We all know of obvious distortions of reality
based on cruel, paranoid, or untrustworthy parents
whose child, later an adult, will experience people
and the world as extensions of this earlier distortion.
Overly protective, smothering parents
can jell their child's psyche
to be a dependent, easily intimidated, and unaggressive one.
We know from experience, however, that another child
with the same parents can grow up
to be the opposite, or at least very different.
Still, a general statement is possible:
Ultimately, we are indeed the product of our childhood
and the parental "imago"—the way we perceived our parents.

The therapist's role is to help the patient
assume responsibility for how he or she
is and can become.

Transference can be spiritual or divine—that is, numinous.
But transference can occur to an institution,
a place, a city, a nation, a race. It can also be demonic.
Transference in people who have been abused or
who have suffered catastrophic trauma,
rape, violence, torture, incest, and terrorism
is grounded in the here-and-now actuality of the events.
Unless the analyst understands and deals with the actual
experience, treatment can flounder and fail,
or even be an additional trauma.

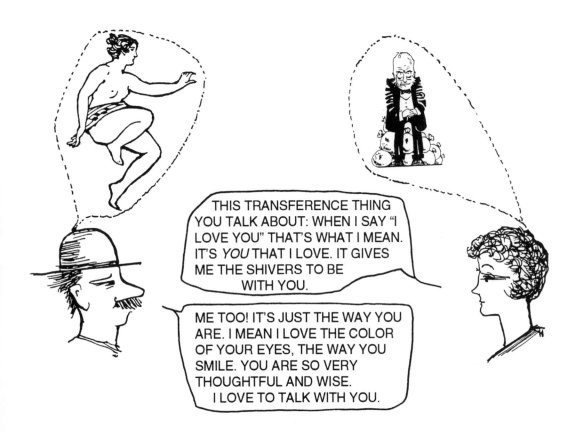

A Dialogue with a Patient Illustrating Transference/ Countertransference

I had worked with the patient for five years.
Her panic, anxiety, and depression were gone.
Her agoraphobia was diminished.
Her spirits, which had been dark and scary, were cheerful.
Her life had come out of darkness into light.
She had worked hard and faithfully at her therapy.

The time approached to end her treatment.
About four months previously, my book *Practical Jung*
had been published. I suggested that she buy a copy.
She said she would.
I fantasized that she had immediately purchased it
and read it at once from cover to cover.

Months passed and she never mentioned my book.
From time to time, I thought she would
tell me how much she liked it and learned from it.

One day, as I was talking to her about ending her therapy,
she told me she had been reading a book that she liked.
It was a mystery story. I felt hurt.
Although it was not smart of me, I asked her,
"Have you read my book?"
"No," she answered indifferently, adding as an afterthought,
"I was going to buy it, but I was too busy."

"I don't think so," I replied.

I thought that her unconscious
had kept her from getting my book
to protect her from fostering
my pride and sense of power.
She was silent for a long time.
We looked at each other.
It was an awkward, but strangely pleasant interlude.
The wordless interval was warm and expressive of understanding.
She smiled and said,
"Then why do you think I haven't bought it?"
"Guess."

She replied, "Well, I procrastinate, you know."
"I know, but that's not the answer."
"Well, maybe your book would help me."
A statement and a question.
"It might."
"Or maybe," she went on, "it would give me some insight
        into how you think."

A bell rang in my mind.
"You *know* how I think," I responded.
"Oh yes, of course. Maybe it would tell me more about you."
A second bell rang in my mind.
I was beginning to understand and realize she also understood.
I tried to express my thoughts,
"You see, by *not* buying my book
you're saying that you *don't* want to know more about me.
That you want to be less closely tied and dependent.
It seems to me that you want things to continue just as
they have been going."

She was silent and thoughtful.
"Ah yes." A light sparked in her eyes. "I think so."
She paused, and as if not to hurt my feelings added,
"*But* I'll get your book!"
"That's not the point."
"I know."
"You get the point."
And then we spoke about tapering off her appointments
and the time she would stop coming to see me.

It was then that I felt a sadness.
I understood that her not buying my book
was a subtle testimonial to me
as if I didn't need her affirmation.
Sadness told me that my countertransference feeling
was such that a part of me didn't want her to leave
or the analysis to end. That realization was liberating.

Another Transference/Countertransference Dialogue

As therapy is coming to an end:

PATIENT: Is that your Rolls Royce in the parking lot?

ME: You're kidding.

PATIENT: No. I'm serious. Is that your Rolls Royce?

ME: You think you've psyched me out. [Laughing]

PATIENT: I know your real feelings toward me. You try to hide them! You hide behind your professional dignity, but you really want me. You can't let me go. You show it. You feel about me exactly as I feel about you, but you're afraid to admit it. Go ahead—admit it! [Said with some passion.]

[silence]

You like expensive things! I know. Look at your office.

ME: You think you know me. And you think I own a Rolls Royce.

PATIENT: Yes.

ME: Not mine.

PATIENT: [Changing the subject, asking for something related to the doctor's professional role—testing me.] Would you write me a prescription for this? [Hands me an advertisement for a vitamin product.]

ME: No.

PATIENT: I don't understand. You mean you won't? If I asked you for a tranquilizer, you would.

ME: No, I would not. Not unless I thought you needed it. Like I did two years ago for your phobia and panic. When the phobia went away, you stopped taking the tranquilizer.

PATIENT: If I wanted *marijuana* and asked you, you would give it to me.

ME: [Losing patience with her provocative demanding, I answered in a deliberate challenge.] Try.

PATIENT: I had a chance last week and I didn't take it.

ME: You're avoiding the question because you know my answer. [Interpretive paraphrase] Would I give you anything you asked for?

[Total silence lasting almost five minutes, the longest pause of any time in her therapy. The dialogue changes dramatically.]

PATIENT: For the first time in years, my husband and I have been really talking. I don't know where all the anger went. It's an unbelievable feeling of relief. Suddenly I feel very close. [This was surprising.]

ME: Just a minute. This might be far off, or it might be right on the button. You asked me for a prescription. You more or less ordered me to give it to you. You began to analyze me and interpret my feelings. But you were, I think, asking me to say *no* because you are actually closer to your husband and because your life is at last working out so well in so many ways. But you have given up your feelings about me as the great rich doctor with a Rolls Royce who is in love with you and afraid to admit it. You knew I wasn't going to give you any magic pills because I don't believe in drugs on demand, or in the love you wanted. *That's the point!* You don't actually want it because you don't need it to counterbalance the hatred you used to have for your husband.

PATIENT: [Pause] I think for the first time since our last appointment three weeks ago when we were talking about termination of therapy that I have felt I don't have to come here every week. Not even that idea sends shivers down my spine.

ME: Yes. Next time when we meet three weeks from now, we can talk about when we can stop.

After she left, I thought to myself that she was reluctant to leave her fantasy doctor whom she projected onto me and was, at the same time, wondering if I could bear to leave her. The dialogue is more than just banter. Thus, it was possible for her to free herself from self-defeating, destructive, and seductive behavior by which she had gotten her way in the past. It seemed to me that when she could withdraw her projections from me, she could rekindle her love for her husband. The transference love was based in part on a real feeling of closeness and love, but mostly on projection. It was like enacting a would-be affair so that she could give up the fantasy for the reality.

It is often the case that a patient and a therapist get caught up in identifying who is who in the transference when the image is non-specific. For example, in classical psychoanalysis, whoever seems to have the qualities of the analyst is interpreted in a reductive manner as representing the real analyst and the specific parental *imago*. It is my experience that if the therapist jumps to this conclusion he or she is apt to end up with a narcissistic intrusion where feelings and authority wipe away many other possibilities. In this instance, the analyst becomes an omnipresent dream figure. This was the basis for the early predominance of transference analysis in the Freudian school. In Jungian psychology the dream analyst is very likely to represent that patient's repertoire of inner analysts. This facilitates the patient's autonomy and responsibility.

It is safe to say that on many occasions, a transference figure can be thought of as representing a class or genus of person or objects. By specifically identifying the image as "generic," doors may open rather than close:

PATIENT: Every time I see my previous therapist I get furious. Even now I keep thinking how he would put words in my mouth all the time. He would say, "That's me in your dream," or "You think. . . ." I would challenge him and say, "No! It's me," or "I don't think that." He would respond by analyzing the resistance and refusing to consider my thoughts, my truth. So I gave up and when he would say, "You think . . ." and "Don't you think . . ." or "It is me. . . ." I would say "Yes."

ME: You could have said, "No."

PATIENT: You don't understand. It was like my father. He would order me to behave as he dictated. He would do awful things. He wouldn't let me go. And that is the way it was with my husband. I wanted to get away, but he wouldn't let me go until I just couldn't stand it another moment. I ran away.

ME: Ran away to your father.

PATIENT: I was desperate. I know it was an Oedipal problem but what does that do to help me? I've worked on that one. My former therapist would say, "But you haven't worked through it." How in the hell could I work through it—whatever that means— with my therapist telling me what I thought and who was who? I finally had to submit and agree to go along with what he said.

ME: I know, to stop the torment, or so you thought. We have worked with the Jungian concept of being caught in a complex; the good little compliant girl, the *puella aeternus*. We've looked at the archetypal image of the Terrible Father, the destroyer, but that didn't help much. Every time this autocratic paternalistic man appears . . .

PATIENT: Yesterday I was so furious at a man who was . . . Oh, God, will it ever stop?

ME: We have worked with this I–It for a long time. It is as if you have been imprisoned by it. Perhaps a dream might help.

PATIENT: I didn't recall a single dream this week, but as you were talking I kept thinking of that nightmare when I was four years old, the one I told you recurred for many years about a German soldier who was chasing me. All I could see of him was his boots. I hid in the closet and locked the door. He stood outside. I knew if I stayed in the closet I would die, and if I opened the door I would face this huge animal man. I was caught. I would wake up terrified. I now know what that was about.

ME: It is like a post-traumatic nightmare. But giving it that label won't help. If we look at the enemy, not as a soldier, doctor, husband, man, father, but as a common idea and reduce it to a simple image, it might offer you a "way out."

PATIENT: Like what? Archetype, fairy story, myth?

ME: No. Chemistry.

PATIENT: Chemistry as the answer, from you? They'll throw you out of the Jungian Club.

ME: By chemistry I mean what I call generic transference, using the word *generic*, as when I write a prescription for a specific drug. Instead of writing the trade name and paying a high charge for the advertising, packaging, and salesmanship, the patient pays less for the same chemical sold as a generic drug. The treatment is to use the same pattern of molecules by chemical name, and not pay the price for a "brand named drug."

PATIENT: You are just substituting another name by "generic" transference.

ME: Not really. By leaving all the elaborate labels and packaging aside, you get the identical thing without paying the price for a fancy name.

PATIENT: The "real" drug would help just like the generic. So what's the point?

ME: The point is that the common denominator is the same everywhere, all over the world and not dressed up in this country or that by a code name. Can you grasp the idea that the father, the husband, the German soldier, the therapist, and this other man are all the same chemistry? It is an I–It relationship not an I–Thou. Try to forget analyzing each disguise in which the monster comes; think of dumping them in the same bottles of chemicals. Don't forget to screw the lids on. This might just give you a mental image in which you can discard these thoughts, like the philosopher who learned to drop his intrusive thoughts into an imaginary dump.

PATIENT: Like my Macintosh computer. It has an image of a garbage can and I can eliminate anything on the screen by dumping it in the can, which actually gets bigger the more I put into it.

ME: Yes. That is objectifying a feeling to deal with it. It is akin to Active Imagination. After all, we are basically all the same chemicals—cognitive therapy, huh?

PATIENT: Isn't that a cop-out?

ME: Why? Like Berthold Brecht said, "Grub first, then ethics."

PATIENT: Sounds cynical and greedy.

ME: Like healthy selfishness. *Not* fighting every dark force that comes terrifying you in one guise or another could be the better part of wisdom. Dump them in the garbage can.

PATIENT: So that is what you mean by generic transference.

ME: It is the same in dreams. Suppose you dream of "a doctor." It would be a generic doctor.

PATIENT: Could be you, same chemistry or someone else, or even me, I suppose.

ME: Yes. By calling it "generic" we use a new and fresh metaphor. For now that is a fresh idea. Later, like most metaphors over time, it will be a dead metaphor which becomes dull and lifeless.

PATIENT: Are you inferring that there is a Generic Archetype?

ME: You will make me a card carrying Jungian analyst one way or the other. Chemistry! Not alchemy, not archetypes. It is a nonproprietary name for a whole class of things. It is not a trademark. It gets down to the nitty gritty, the periodic table of elements, of which there are just so many and no more in the universe.

PATIENT: So how does all that talk help me when I see that man tomorrow?

ME: Call out your mental computer with the garbage can.

ELEVEN

Possessed by an Archetype

You must be kidding.
　　　Possessed by an archetype!
　　　　Possessed??
You're back into the Middle Ages.
　　　　　You are positively medieval.
You're talking magic and spells.
　　　We are in the *Age of Science.*
No one, but no one, talks of being possessed.

I do.
Poets do.
Artists and writers do.
Theologians do.
General Motors has a Repossession Division.
Jungians do, wide awake and conscious.
They even do it in their sleep and their dreams.

It would be more appropriate
to use another term.
Otherwise we might have to call in an
Exorcist.
Right?

It happens in fairy tales and legends,
in the movies and in primitive societies
even now. They do.
Yes, but they are backward.
Yes, but—you are not?
Jung spoke of the occult and he
studied it.
For shame! In the twentieth century.
What will your respectable colleagues
think of you?
Possessed by an archetype.
　　　By an archetype!
　　　By an archetype!

They will be thinking in their dreams
just like I am, only they won't recognize
an archetype when they see one.
But, but of course not. They don't believe in them.

Then we shall call it something else and give
a medicinal potion which will heal
the virus that is going around.
                    You know. Everybody has it.
                    It's going around.
                    My doctor said it was a virus.

Yes.
Yes.

It is *our possessions* that we guard, right?
It is against the law to steal my possessions. Right?
Right.
Every possession is not a material object. Is it?
An idea can be in your possession. Can't it?
Then why can't *you* be in the possession of something
                    that I choose to call an archetype?

OK. OK. I give up.
Call it Limburger cheese. Call it haddock's eyes.
Call it what you will, but the scientific name for it
is Illusion, Delusion, Hallucination, or Madness.
It's all in your mind. It's not real.

It is, indeed, in your mind.
It is, however, quite real.

NAME THE THING!

"The name of the song is called 'Haddock's Eyes.' "
"Oh, that's the name of the song, is it?" Alice said, trying to feel interested.
"No, you don't understand," the Knight said, looking a little vexed. "That's what the name is called. The name really is 'The Aged, Aged Man.' "
"Then I ought to have said, 'That's what the song is called,' " Alice corrected herself.
"No, you oughtn't, that's another thing. The song is called 'Ways and Means,' but that's only what it's called, you know!" (Carroll 1982, pp. 226–227)

Lewis Carroll

Archetypes and Numbers

Where do the numbers come from? Who discovered them anyway? They are both mysterious and the ultimate expression of the finite. What is a cipher—nothing or everything in itself? You can't say that if I've seen *one*, too, I've seen all ones, or toos or twos. What is the mythology of numbers and what has it got to do with *Understandable Jung*?

A lot.

Numbers are archetypes, and they appear in our dreams, images, and visions. Numbers can hold a power over us. People have even been known to die for a number.

Much is known about numbers from empirical experience.

When Jung first discovered the concept of *archetypes*, he called them "primordial images" and described them as if they were nodal points in a supersaturated liquid, which is the nidus for the formation of a specific crystal form. Out of the mother liquor is born the predetermined geometrically shaped crystal, which has an unmistakable identity but nonetheless

[The conscious mind] knows "spirit" always seems to come from above, while from below comes everything that is sordid and worthless. For people who think in this way, spirit means highest freedom, a soaring over the depths, deliverance from the prison of the chthonic world, and hence a refuge for all those timorous souls who do not want to become anything different. But water is earthy and tangible, it is also the fluid of the instinct-driven body, blood and the flowing of blood, the odour of the beast, carnality heavy with passion. The unconscious is the psyche that reaches down from the daylight of mentally and morally lucid consciousness into the nervous system that for ages has been known as the "sympathetic." This does not govern perception and muscular activity like the cerebrospinal system, and thus control the environment; but, though functioning without sense-organs, it maintains the balance of life and, through the mysterious paths of sympathetic excitation, not only gives us knowledge of the innermost life of other beings but also has an inner effect upon them. (Jung 1954b, par. 41)

JUNG

appears in a wide variety of shapes. This is like the archetype that is only a potential for a specific form, psychic instinct, instinctual behavior or image, which is manifest in an infinite number of symbols.

The archetype itself is nothing. *No one ever saw an archetype. Remember that, please*! Or a nodal point that can be known only when it crystallizes as something else.

Certain numbers seem to have more or less predictable meaning in the psyche, such as 1 being unity and wholeness; 2 being division, tension, and separation; 3 being the number of movement and change; 4 the number of wholeness; 0 is the beginning; and 5 is the quintessence, being 4 + 1.

Jung was so intensely involved with the meaning of the number 4 and its description as quaternity that some critics thought he was a quaternity pusher. But history bears him out. The endless repetition of the number 4 as complete and whole in cultures of all ages qualifies it as an archetype. For example, in medieval times, the universe was said to be composed of four elements: fire, water, air, and earth. The quaternity is the logical balance of any whole judgment; the four quarters of the earth, sky or any circle, and the four ways of spiritual development. A basic tenet of analytical psychology is typology with the *four functions:* thinking, feeling, intuition, and sensation. The idea of completeness is the circle or sphere, but its natural division is quaternity.

The mandala (magic circle) is characterized by four entry/exit points, like the four rivers of the Garden of Eden. The mystery of numbers is a joy that warms the heart of any Jungian, but a consternation to anyone who "likes to live by the numbers," which is supposed to wipe out any mystery and uncertainty. Like painting by the numbers.

Stop! Stop! Enough of your lecture. I get the idea! What I want is to understand how numbers affect my psyche. Is this number business going to help me understand anything except theory? I need to get my teeth into something solid like how to get an unlisted number.

O.K.

Nobody's Business

The trickster is the personification of the shadow archetype who appears in many guises. I will illustrate the trickster in a series of sketches and dialogues.

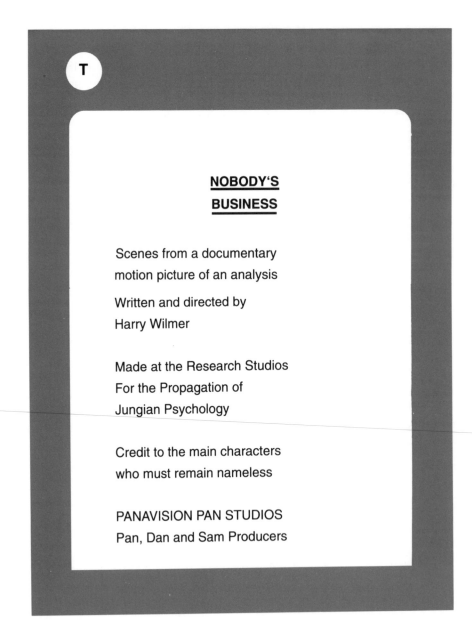

T

NOBODY'S
BUSINESS

Scenes from a documentary
motion picture of an analysis

Written and directed by
Harry Wilmer

Made at the Research Studios
For the Propagation of
Jungian Psychology

Credit to the main characters
who must remain nameless

PANAVISION PAN STUDIOS
Pan, Dan and Sam Producers

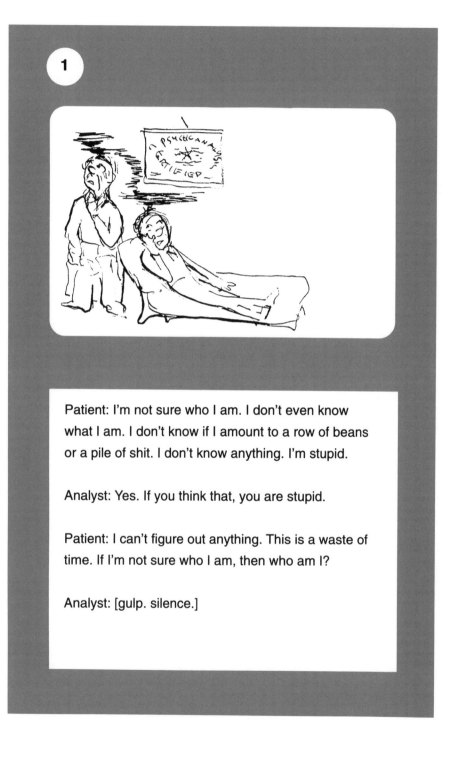

Patient: I'm not sure who I am. I don't even know what I am. I don't know if I amount to a row of beans or a pile of shit. I don't know anything. I'm stupid.

Analyst: Yes. If you think that, you are stupid.

Patient: I can't figure out anything. This is a waste of time. If I'm not sure who I am, then who am I?

Analyst: [gulp. silence.]

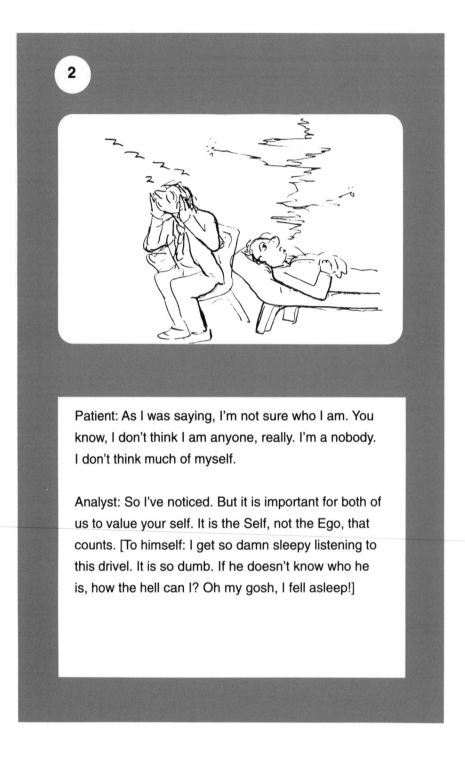

Patient: As I was saying, I'm not sure who I am. You know, I don't think I am anyone, really. I'm a nobody. I don't think much of myself.

Analyst: So I've noticed. But it is important for both of us to value your self. It is the Self, not the Ego, that counts. [To himself: I get so damn sleepy listening to this drivel. It is so dumb. If he doesn't know who he is, how the hell can I? Oh my gosh, I fell asleep!]

3

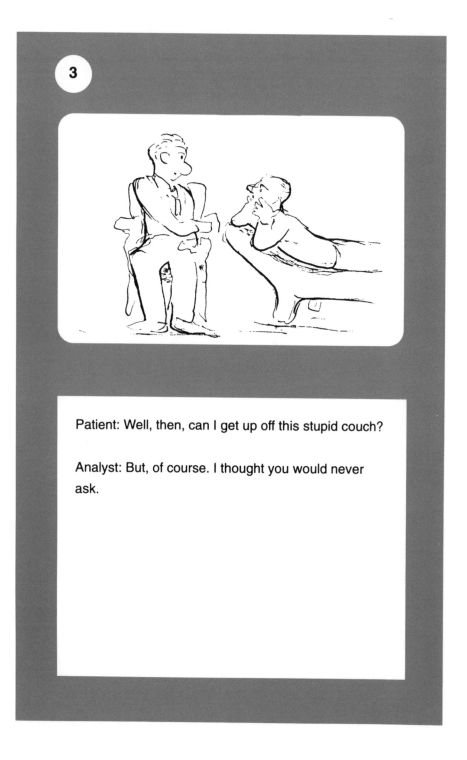

Patient: Well, then, can I get up off this stupid couch?

Analyst: But, of course. I thought you would never ask.

Patient: Where did my analyst go?

Trickster: He took a powder. I am his associate.

Patient: I don't want to talk to you!

Trickster: To whom do you think you have been talking all this time? *And so*—can I help you? What's going through your mind?

Patient: I have been thinking how good things were in the past. It was a golden time. I had everything. Why has it all changed? Why? If only. . . .

5

Trickster: Oh no . . . not that again! Not that garbage. You are living in the *hic et nunc!*

Patient: The what? The *hic et nunc?* Sounds like a comedy team.

Trickster: A little mirth doesn't hurt the *hic et nunc*. They are the here and now. Today. Today is forever.

Patient: Then I've got to get going quick before tomorrow. What am I doing here?

Trickster: Beats me.

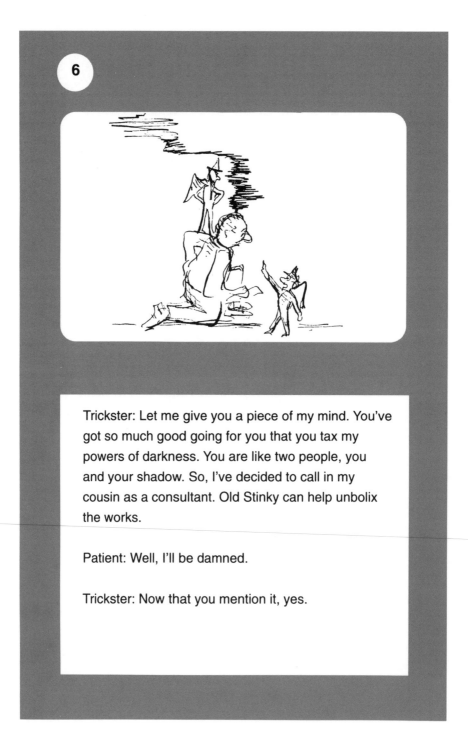

Trickster: Let me give you a piece of my mind. You've got so much good going for you that you tax my powers of darkness. You are like two people, you and your shadow. So, I've decided to call in my cousin as a consultant. Old Stinky can help unbolix the works.

Patient: Well, I'll be damned.

Trickster: Now that you mention it, yes.

7

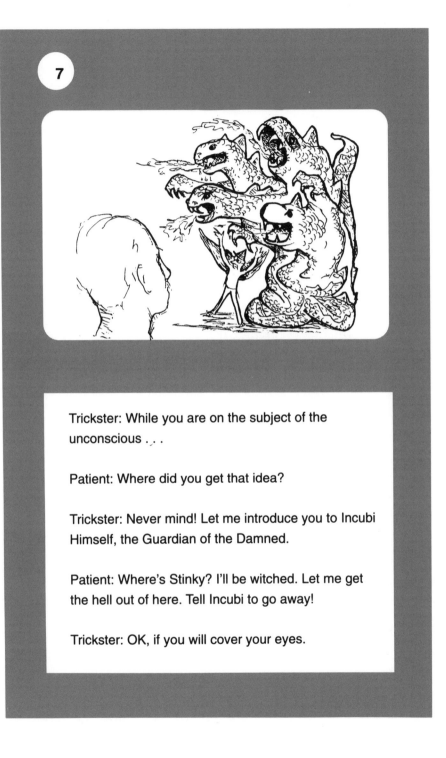

Trickster: While you are on the subject of the unconscious . . .

Patient: Where did you get that idea?

Trickster: Never mind! Let me introduce you to Incubi Himself, the Guardian of the Damned.

Patient: Where's Stinky? I'll be witched. Let me get the hell out of here. Tell Incubi to go away!

Trickster: OK, if you will cover your eyes.

Trickster: Now I will say the magic word: GO! Old Inky is gone in a puff.

Patient: Is that all you have to do, say GO!?

Trickster: That's all you have to do. Now open your eyes, and I'll be gone, too. Oh, I'll be here. I'll just be invisible.

9

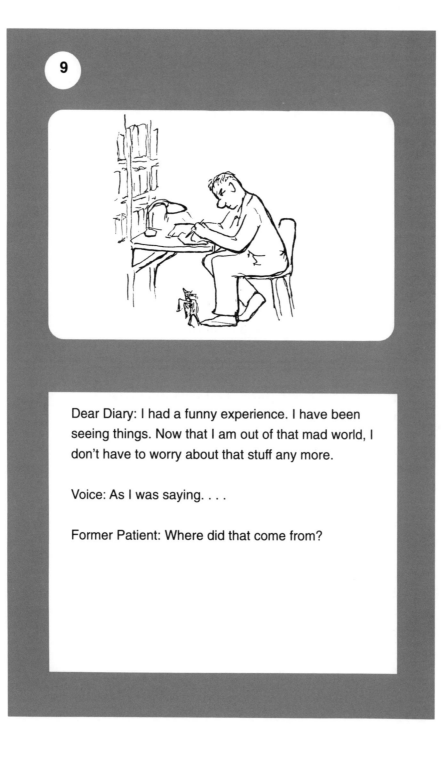

Dear Diary: I had a funny experience. I have been seeing things. Now that I am out of that mad world, I don't have to worry about that stuff any more.

Voice: As I was saying. . . .

Former Patient: Where did that come from?

The Wounded Healer

About this archetype whom I met firsthand,
The Wounded Healer.
It is safe to say that
no one can heal the psychic wounds of another
unless the healer has healed his or her own wounds.
Each one of us is wounded.
Few like to admit, as if it is shameful.
It is not.
We are all kin to the wounded hero.

Each of us lives out some variation of the hero myth.
Our psychic wounds, denied and ignored, may fester
and disable us, or even lead to our death.
And there are wounds that never heal.

The human condition is such that
we have psychological and biological powers to master our wounds.
If this were not so, humankind would long ago
have gone down the drain.
Out of suffering, failures, and woundedness
comes our character, resilience, and wisdom.

The Wounded Healer archetype, like all archetypes, is
transpersonal and connects our pain, suffering, and despair with humanity.
We are all wounded.

In the collective unconscious, each one of us embodies the
archetype of the wounded healer.
The myth of the Wounded Healer relates to a unique or
special wound that by some miraculous or superhuman experience,
like Parsifal and the Holy Grail, Amphortis, the wounded
king, is healed, thereby transforming the world.

The Vocation of Healing

This healer ranges from the mystic and the shamanic to the mother, father, helper, and the one called to be a healer, doctor, or priest. This vocation or *calling* is the experience that sets apart the one with spiritual power from the technician.

Let us take the *shaman* of primitive cultures.

Having suffered, the shaman has experienced powers to go into trances and to journey to the sky or the underworld, to heal with rituals and with the power to overcome evil. Such shamanistic incantations and ceremonials are relived today in rituals that are modernized, sanitized, and rationalized. The shaman's life is one of isolation, stress, suffering, and curing. The shaman can take into himself the suffering and illness and woundedness of another. This is known in the helping profession when the healer identifies with the wounded by becoming the wounded one and paying the price.

This unity of healer and sufferer depotentiates the poison or evil spirits and thus makes the shaman an awesome, mysterious person. Perhaps this mysterious projection of magician gives the healer's persona its awesome power. In ancient times, people made pilgrimages to shrines; in modern times, we call our sacred healing places by the names of the gods of science or the *Center* which carries numinous or divine power.

A tragedy of our times is that healing has become a business, and patients, or pilgrims, have become customers. There is a war between the "provider," the consumer, and the euphemistic "third-party." The lawyers, the insurance companies, and the government have swallowed the consumer up.

When I was an intern, I developed tuberculosis. A year of strict bed rest was required. An interesting thing happened to me in the sanatorium. One day, out of the blue, the words "Huber the Tuber" came to me. I imagined a tubercle bacillus inside me causing all this trouble, and his name was Huber the Tuber. As I lay motionless for long periods of time, a fantasy began to weave its story in my mind. I saw it in images, and the words followed the pictures. In as much as all activity was prohibited, I took to drawing secretly the pictures of my story, what I called "Huber the Tuber: The Lives and Loves of a Tubercle Bacillus."

Each day, I drew one picture in a sketchbook and wrote the brief story of how Huber came into my lungs, built his home, fell in love with Bovey, a bovine tubercle bacillus whom he met by the Old Blood Stream, and had an encounter with evil. The hero of the story, Huber, met Nasty von Sputum. After a long, harrowing journey through Lungland, the White Cells finally triumphed, and Huber lay a dormant prisoner in an air cell lined with calcium blocks drained from the blood of the capillary arterioles. The story and cartoon drawings were funny, and soon the

National Tuberculosis Association (now the American Lung Association) published it in a cloth-bound book. It turned out to be a best-seller.

The book is a spontaneous discovery of what Jung called "active imagination," of which I knew nothing at the time. Jung recommended that at some point in analysis his patients write, draw, dance, or create an evolving fantasy under the direction of the ego, which allows the unconscious to be objectified.

Huber the Tuber occurred in an imaginary place with imaginary people or objects.

It was, indeed, an individuation myth for me. It was the myth of the hero, as a positive shadow invader who overcomes evil in the form of Nasty von Sputum. The book was written in 1941, and some of its images came from World War II. It all took place inside my chest as psyche.

It is an archetypal story of the Myth of the Hero.

After Huber has won the attention of all the Tubers, he told them, "Don't blow a cavity, don't cut up the lung. Everyone can have an airsac to himself. Chew slowly, enjoy yourself, and eat yourself out of house and home! So, my friends, build homes of calcium stones and all will be well." They all started working and soon the Tubers settled down in the calcified section.

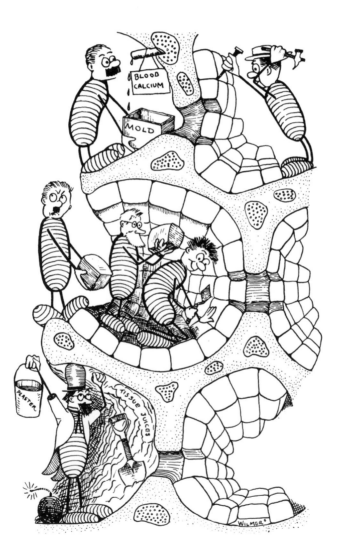

Huber came to "Unter den Cavity nr.3" which formed a great natural amphitheater. Long banners hung behind the speakers' platform. On them was "S. K." which stood for Spitzkrieg. A great shout arose as Nasty entered. He began to speak and the audience became deathly silent. "Parachutists," he roared, "We are about to shoot you from the special Tuber-Shooting gun! You will leave Lungland, travel up the airways, turn right and go out the windpipe. *Go forth and infiltrate!* Eat all the lung you can."

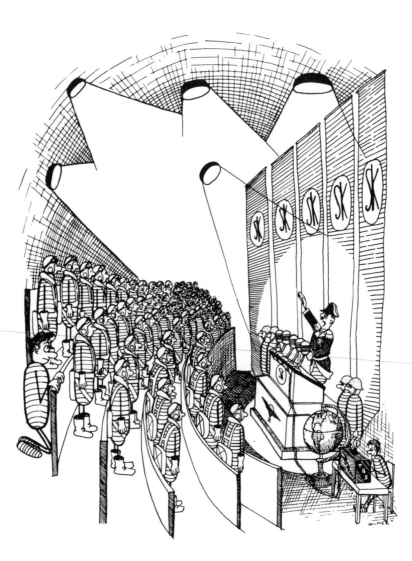

The chief of the White Cell Home Guard summoned all his army together and there was great celebration. Bagpipes, with their squeaks and wheezes, drums with their booming, horns with their "oom opah pah," and trumpeters with their clarion calls announced the end of the war. "VICTORY, VICTORY, VICTORY! It is ours! We have defeated the Tubers. Those who we have not killed are our prisoners of war. So long was we keep them in jail . . . then Lungland is free. LONG LIVE LUNGLAND!"

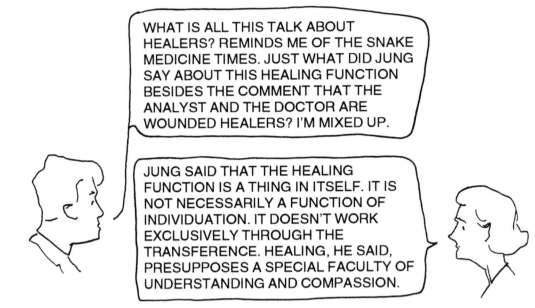

WHAT IS ALL THIS TALK ABOUT HEALERS? REMINDS ME OF THE SNAKE MEDICINE TIMES. JUST WHAT DID JUNG SAY ABOUT THIS HEALING FUNCTION BESIDES THE COMMENT THAT THE ANALYST AND THE DOCTOR ARE WOUNDED HEALERS? I'M MIXED UP.

JUNG SAID THAT THE HEALING FUNCTION IS A THING IN ITSELF. IT IS NOT NECESSARILY A FUNCTION OF INDIVIDUATION. IT DOESN'T WORK EXCLUSIVELY THROUGH THE TRANSFERENCE. HEALING, HE SAID, PRESUPPOSES A SPECIAL FACULTY OF UNDERSTANDING AND COMPASSION.

When I was an intern at Gorgas Hospital in Panama in 1940,
one of our services had been at a nearby leprosarium.
At the time, there were no drugs to treat leprosy.
The lepers languished in screened-in houses.
Their faces, hands, and feet were mutilated.
At that time, there were no drugs to treat tuberculosis.
The only "cure" was strict bed rest in a sanatorium.
The tubercle bacillus looks like the leprosy bacillus.

Tuberculosis was still called "The Captain of Death."
It frequently killed medical students, nurses, and doctors.
It was more contagious than leprosy.

My encounters with death and near-death led to strong
feelings of compassion and empathy for individuals
who were struck down with disease and suffering.

My encounter enhanced my dedication to being a physician.
It reinforced my vocation or calling to be a doctor.
Lying still, being confined to bed,
forced me to confront my inner world.
My outer life was confined to the world around my bed,
within the walls of a hospital.
I knew the meaning of "Physician, heal thyself."
I had met the archetype of the wounded healer:
in my physician and myself.

God and *Imago Dei*

Jung said that religion itself was a part of the collective psyche rather than a neurotic illusion as Freud claimed, having traced it to the father. When I was a professor of psychiatry at the University of Texas Health Science Center in San Antonio, the analytic faculty consisted of a Freudian analyst and a Jungian analyst. At a case conference, I spoke of the frequent religious conflicts that my patients experienced. To my astonishment my Freudian colleague replied that he had never seen a patient with a religious conflict.

When I suggested that perhaps he called these conflicts by a different name (i.e., oedipal complex), he shrugged his shoulders and said that was not a religious problem.

When my schizophrenic patients described their delusions of God and Satan, I did not immediately rush for the neuroleptic drugs but asked them to talk about the God and devil that they saw and heard. That way, I learned a lot about the collective unconscious and psychic reality.

Am I to tell someone else that their God is not their God? Or were they the same? Was this not the *imago Dei* in pure culture—that is, the archetypal image of God? Was this not the primal battle between good and evil? The drugs for schizophrenia control the symptoms and usually are necessary, but they also create in the patient thinking that is more acceptable to doctors and staff who can then cease worrying about the patient being "possessed" by demons and gods. Instead, they can call it delusion and make wonderful connections to the patient's childhood. But relationship exists among religion, spirit, soul, and psychology.

Perhaps Jung's most significant work on this subject was his book, *Answer to Job.* Jung postulated that God has two sides, a satanic or dark force, and a numinous or divine side, and that we cannot understand the divine without the demonic and vice versa. These are the polar opposites of the single archetype of the Self, of *imago Dei,* that is, the image of God, not the theology. The all-loving god was one aspect of God. Would an all-loving god allow the pain, cruelty, suffering, and evil in the world? Jung once spoke of himself as a heretic who, in the Middle Ages, would have been burned at the stake.

Where do such images come from? How did people in the Western world deal with them in the past? The medieval world was dominated by demons, monsters, satanic forces, angels, and God. People not only believed in them, they knew them and talked with them. Our conscious psyche has moved beyond such stages, but where did all the devils, demons, and monsters go? They didn't go anywhere. They remained in the collective unconscious where they have always been. They now emerge in accordance with our contemporary culture—in our cinema, television, literature, the arts, and in dreams, visions, and madness.

Jung was indignant with people who thought he believed that the God-image was the same as God. He wrote to a pastor:

> You write, apparently without any misgivings, that I equate God with the self. You seem not to have noticed that I speak of the *God-image and not of God* because it is quite beyond me to say anything about God at all. It is more than astonishing that you have failed to perceive this fundamental distinction, it is shattering. I don't know what you must take me for if you can impute such stupidities to me . . . (1955, p. 260).

Even with the atheistic rejection of God, there is an image to reject, and always something fills that void—something to worship or possess our belief system, which may be the non-God. It is then one belief pitted against another.

What About God Dreams?

Perfectly ordinary people dream of God. What do you say about that if you accept the manifest dream as the dream and not something disguised?

A patient tells me this dream:

Part I

> *I go into a theater and inside I experience seeing God. I cannot explain or describe it, but it is a great powerful vision that affects me deeply. I go outside the theater and my little boy is there, and he wants to go into the theater to see what I have seen. I take him in, but instead of the God image, he sees a mural with small notices being added. In the middle of one is my picture. I know that it means I am going to die and that my son will leave me and I will never see him again.*

Jung said that he didn't need to believe in God because "I know." What he was saying was that he knew of the existence of God-images and that the experience of God was a universal experience. When he was asked why should you call this something "God," he said, "Why not. It's always been called 'God.' " What has this got to do with archetypes?

The God-image, or *imago Dei,* he was talking about is the central archetype, which he called the *Self*. That is *not* a metaphysical God, but that which embodies all of the psyche, both conscious and unconscious. He did say that God and the self appeared to be identical. So he got in a lot of hot water with the theologians.

So what else is new?

---

*(Jung 1959, pp. 522–523)
**(Jung 1955, p. 265)

This powerful, sad dream evoked the deep feelings that characterize archetypal dreams. The dream forced him to look at his own mortality and religious feelings. That it took place in a motion-picture theater suggested to me that this was a projection, which is how we see the picture in the theater. The dream does not mean the actual death of the father except as an ultimate event, because dreams of actual death are different. The dream ends with this sequence:

Part II

The scene changes and I set my dream book down by the street. But then I go back and pick it up and put it in the mailbox. The weather is beautiful. The sun is bright. I feel good.

Although he discards his dream diary in the street, he returns to pick it up and mail it. He deposits it in a safe container and when he does so, he sees the bright light of day in the outside world.

The above dream about God and death had a *numinous* quality— that is, a divine aura or a power that casts a spell. In ancient Rome, when a new town was built, a stone was placed in the center and was called the *numen*. It was the *numen* that accounted for the attraction to the place. We all have numinous places to which we are drawn, our special places on the earth, or what we must see or experience. It is a religious experience such as being in Chartres Cathedral, the pilgrimage to Mecca, the Black Madonna at Einsiedeln in Switzerland, Jerusalem, Lourdes, and the holy mountains. The *numinosum* is the phenomenon that is the source of the numinous radiation and attraction.

The Central Archetype

Jung's concept of the Self may be among his most important contributions. The Self is supraordinate to consciousness and to both the personal and collective unconscious. Jung conceptualized the Self as *imago Dei,* which can appear in many symbolic manifestations.

We know about the personal unconscious from Freud and the collective unconscious from Jung. The Self, which encompasses both consciousness and the unconscious, is the totality of the psyche. We can ask, "What is the point of making an abstract identification of such a supraordinate force and calling it an archetype?" One might say, why do we call a mountain a mountain? Because it exists, and in our language it exists as a mountain.

Many people describe their mothers or fathers in demonic terms or like monsters. Many parents are monsters to children. Some parents were so maligned and abused as children themselves that they are still possessed by the Devouring or Terrible Mother or Father archetype.

The Jungian concept of the Self is unrelated to "self-psychology," where the term *self* means the individual being, as himself or herself, or an object in object-relations constructs. Jung's hypothetical Self has a mysterious, even spirit force. However, such comments leave scientific and academic psychologists and psychiatrists ice cold.

We might look at the Zen concept of the Self as a widely appreciated nonscientific system:

> Since the awakening of consciousness, the human mind has acquired the habit of thinking dichotomously. In fact, thinking is in itself so characterized, for without opposition of subject and object, no thinking can take place. . . . The result is that the intellectually dichotomized self is placed above and over the underlying one which is the true absolute Self transcending all discriminatory distinction. We must come to this Self and personally "interview" it if we really desire to get settled at the final abode of our being. As this ultimate Self is above all forms of dichotomy, it is neither inner nor outer, neither metaphysical nor psychological, neither objective nor subjective. If the term "Self" is misleading, we may designate it as "God" or "Being," "Man" or "the Soul," "Nothing" or anything. (Suzuki 1972, p. 3)

You see, it's like I said, this is not about science and medicine, it's about spooky Eastern religions and airy-fairy things. Humbug!

If Zen bugs you, and you must discard Jung because his ideas are not scientific but myths in the ordinary way people talk about myths, then we can have a nice hermetic system. Hermes . . . ah.

Hermes, guide to the soul, god of revelation, lord of thought (Jung 1944, p. 102).

Persona

The persona is an archetype described by Jung to express the face we turn to the public, of how we wish to appear. It is like the masks worn by the actors and actresses in ancient Greek drama, hence *personae dramatis*. The persona is expressed in all our outer manifestation, dress, demeanor, and the façade. It is also an expression of our role in society. It also hides the inner face of our shadow which is turned inwards and which is an expression of that which we hide.

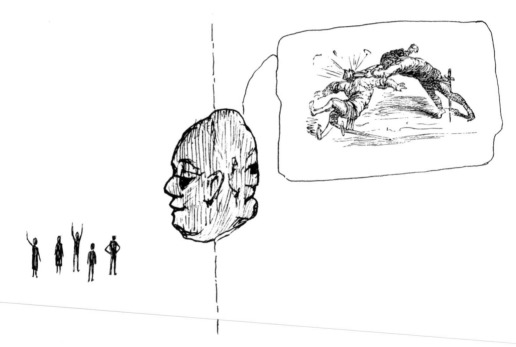

Illustration in balloon from Gustave Dore, Le contres Drolatiques, *1855.*

PERSONA

Swiss National Tourist Office, Zurich

Wild Masquerade in Canton Schwyze—central Switzerland. The "Nusseler" and the "Alte Wyber" (old women) are two carnival figures that appear in the streets on Carnival Monday, dancing to the rhythm of drum beats.

Statue from the Zahringen Fountains, Bern, Switzerland

Some people create their persona to evoke certain projections which are so obvious that they come under the category of disguise.

INFLATION

You are so wonderful that I feel all shivery just looking at you. I don't . . . I can't . . . I don't know how to say this, but . . . . I mean, you know what I want to say . . . ah . . . I love you.

Inflation is the opposite of depression. Often excessive inflation leads to a down period to compensate, the up and down moods. They cycle. You could think of inflation as pride which goeth before the fall. Of the big head. It may, however, just be a passing warm glow of very good feeling that goes with accomplishment, love, and rewards. Euphoria is an overblown inflation and like a balloon it will pop, or it will sweep over other people and give a phony sense of self-importance. It is natural, i.e., human nature to respond instinctually to affirmation so that you appear even more attractive in your mind and in your body. Inflation, when it becomes what is called a "manic defense," hides inferiority feelings and a deep sense of self-worthlessness and depression. However, the simple word *inflation* "blows one's mind."

Inflation

Ah yes, inflation, that up-that-sets-us-up-feeling!
Supergood, Ego-bloated, and Wind-gloated
you can be certain that
always follows,
sooner or later,
deflation and Icarus-like depression.

We live in time of easy highs and awesome lows.
The feel-good, all-is-good, go-for-it,
win-big, windbag, greed, and sham
are hallmarks of our times.

In some measure, they are the stigma of all times,
and according to the Law of Enantiodromia,
in time everything turns into its opposite.
Even now, the wonders of our age are prodigious.

It is inescapable that ups are followed by downs,
that downs are less dangerous than ups,
that there is immense meaning
in the downs of despair, depression, and disillusionment.
From the cauldron of failure,
in the heat of anger and pain,
emerges the possibility of new beginnings.

When the air comes out of inflation,
one comes closer to the earth,
and the healing of the soul.

AS AVA GARDNER SAID,
"DEEP DOWN I'M PRETTY
SUPERFICIAL."

The Museum of Modern Art/Film Stills Archive

The Fall of Babylon

Grandiosity and Inflation: "The Fall of Babylon"

D. W. Griffith, motion picture director, made the film *Intolerance,* anxious to live up to his reputation as the greatest genius of the cinema and to outdo his great financial and critical success, *Birth of a Nation.* This new epic contained the story of Babylon. With thousands of actors and actresses, a grand total of 15,000 persons and 250 chariots, he filmed the scene "The Fall of Babylon."

Said to be the greatest set ever built, walls rose 150 feet and towers higher. Walls were wide and strong enough to hold the weight of racing horses, chariots, and throngs of soldiers in battle scenes. When it opened in 1916, audiences found the film bewildering, confusing, and exhausting. The epic was not a success. Griffith created the entire film without a written script. It was all in his head. It took two years to produce. I think it is safe to say this is an inflation of head and ambition, and its title is not without ironic meanings.

It was truly an epic in the mythology of Hollywood and America. Behind the colossus was a dark shadow, which is the fatal flaw in the myth of the hero, the hubris which leads to the downfall: witness Hollywood (Tucker 1980, p. 387).

The intelligent psychotherapist has known for years that any complicated treatment is an individual, *dialectical* process, in which the doctor, as a person, participates just as much as the patient. . . . The patient, that is to say, can win his own inner security only from the security of his relationship to the doctor as a human being. . . . We could say, without too much exaggeration, that a good half of every treatment that probes at all deeply consists in the doctor's examining himself, for only what he can put right in himself can he hope to put right in the patient. It is no loss, either, if he feels that the patient is hitting him, or even scoring off him: it is his own hurt that gives the measure of his power to heal. This, and nothing else, is the meaning of the Greek myth of the wounded physician. (Jung 1951b, par. 239)

JUNG

Although I am illustrating the Wounded Healer archetype in the case of a physical illness, the wounds may be of any sort, and are usually psychological. The essence of this concept is that we are all wounded, but many people in psychological healing roles refer to the woundedness only in the other person and not in themselves.

PART

TWELVE

AN ANIMA—ANIMUS DIALOGUE

You Can Catch On to Statements and Questions That Don't Mean Anything

Or, How to Win an Argument by Not Saying Anything

WOMAN:	So! You *want* me to fail!
MAN:	No, not really. I'm afraid you will fail if you keep going the way you are.
WOMAN:	Then you think that I *deserve* to fail!
MAN:	Well, if you put it that way, *yes*! I suppose so.
WOMAN:	So! You *want* me to fail!
MAN:	Not before *you* started this asinine argument.
WOMAN:	*ME!*
MAN:	What *were* we talking about?
WOMAN:	You don't *ever* listen to me. You *never* have.
MAN:	(silence)
WOMAN:	Didn't *you* hear me?
MAN:	(silence)
WOMAN:	*Well!*
MAN:	(sulking) You *always* have the last word!
WOMAN:	Why not?
MAN:	(walking away angry, stooped with hurt feelings)
WOMAN:	I wish he would fight back just once.

Baited comments, baited questions.
Always that always and nevers and nevers.
The completely unanswerable accusations.
The opinionated ideas as eternal truths.

When there are arguments like this,
it is not the man and woman themselves talking
but the archetypes within them having a go at it.
Her animus and his anima are screaming at each other.
The real people are listening helplessly to the fight,
furious because they can't get a word in edgewise.
Logic and reason are taboo in this irrational world
of the archetypes.

PROJECTION: ANIMA/ANIMUS

The voice of the animus (the contrasexual unconscious of the feminine) and the voice of the anima (the contrasexual unconscious of the masculine) speak with an identifying rhetoric and posture that Jung characterized in certain ways. When the woman is driven by her animus and the man by his anima, the cat-and-dog fights that occur are quite predictable reactions to each other. It is as if each sex reacts in a manner as a caricature of the other sex, and with sour impersonation of the depreciated mood of the other. These concepts have been challenged, but they can be seen in action in the battle between the sexes.

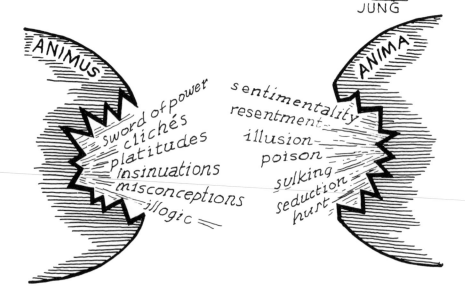

ANIMA-ANIMUS · CAT AND DOG FIGHT

Although men and women unite, they nevertheless represent irreconcilable opposites, which when activated degenerate into deadly hostility.

JUNG

ANIMUS

ANIMA

sword of power
clichés
platitudes
insinuations
misconceptions
illogic

sentimentality
resentment
illusion
poison
sulking
seduction
hurt

The ANIMA/ANIMUS cat-and-dog fights are comprehensible
when you catch onto the idea that the anima and animus
are speaking out of their own stage rhetoric.
The purpose is an attempt of the archetypes
to relate in such a preposterous manner that the real people will
stand up.

The only way to win is to lose,
for the triumph is in mutuality, authenticity,
and generosity of spirit.

(Unaware of the wisdom of triumph in failure, and the success of silence
and nonperpetuation of cat-and-dog fights, the man returns to the room
no longer sulking, but loaded for bear.)

MAN: You know, I don't *really* want you to fail.

WOMAN: Oh God. You don't care!

MAN: Right! You make me mad.

WOMAN: You don't care about me anymore.

MAN: I care. Otherwise, I wouldn't have come back to talk with
            you.

WOMAN: Maybe you would like to care, but you are only interested in
            yourself. You have a mean streak.

MAN: You, too. Everyone does.

WOMAN: That's why you want me to fail.

MAN: Oh, go to hell!

WOMAN: You see what I mean? You admit it!

Sometimes When You Say the Right Thing, It Seems Like the Wrong Thing, But It Isn't

This is a cautionary tale.
It is about therapy that
was moving right along, until one day:

I told her that *pride* was standing in her way.
The next day she called me and left a message:
"I am canceling my next appointment."
I called and suggested that she come back
and talk with me about it. She snapped,
"I don't want to come back at all!"
It might be a good idea anyway, I suggested,
and I hoped she would come back next week
at her regular session and I said no more.

During our last meeting, I had sensed
that she was distressed and angry with me
when I had said that her pride was standing in her way.
She said next, "I am not an ordinary person!"
She was trying to tell me that I should be proud of her,
I guess.
Trying to be philosophical, I had replied,
"We are all ordinary people. All of us."
That had added fuel to the fire, however.

She did come back for her regular hour the following week.
She began at once by complaining:
"You don't talk enough. I do all the talking.
        You are just playing the silent analyst."
I was now silent, but I am not a silent analyst.
It felt as if I was being baited. No matter what I said,
I would be wrong. To me, playing the silent analyst
        is a repulsive game.
Yet here I was, being the silent analyst!
So I said, "Tell me why you wanted to stop seeing me."
She replied,
"Because you never put yourself on the line.
        Only *I* have to do that."

She was an indignant woman standing for equality,
but analysis is not a social equality.
How should I say that when it seemed to me that
I was in hot water for talking too much?
My words about pride had seemed the right thing to say.
It seemed obvious.
Surely she would see how pride goeth before the fall.

Perhaps it was too sharp, too pointed,
telling her that pride was standing in her way.
Her response was to shut me off altogether.
I had not meant to offend her.
What had I not said
after "we are all ordinary people,"
was, "only extraordinary people know that" (Auden 1962, p. 63).

She wanted to be special, to be extraordinary,
and take pride in her projection onto me that I was not ordinary.
Perhaps she wanted to worship that projection she called me.
For to her, if she was special, then I was special
and even more special than she.
This is called love and hate in the transference.

I had offended the image she wanted me to see—that is,
to project onto her.
Its value would be greater, the more special I was.

She went on:
"I *knew* you would call and offer me another appointment
because you are that kind of person."
I cared.
She did indeed know a lot about me,
and was now finding out even more
in this encounter.
Her expression changed and I said,
"You look distressed."
Then, in a statement that totally surprised me,
her anger came out:
"I am because sometimes you take notes,
and sometimes you don't take notes."

You can bet I took a mental note of that!

It had never occurred to me that whether or not
I took notes upset her.
She told me that when I *did* take notes,
she felt that her comments were memorable
because she was saying important things.
When I *didn't* take notes, she was just
being ordinary, and I was not interested.

**Then she confided a dream she had the night that she canceled
her appointment:**

> *I am walking with you on the beach.*
> *The weather is very cold*
> *and the ocean is frozen solid.*
> *I walk out on the ice and it breaks.*
> *You are just standing there watching me.*
> *Then I am wading in the water, which is* warm.
> *I look farther down the beach*
> *and see a gigantic rock with huge waves*
> *breaking against it.*
> *I know that the water around the rock is icy cold,*
> *dark, deep, and dangerous.*
> *I think, "How easily I could drown there."*

She said something had happened,
and she was breaking the ice.
Warmth was beneath the surface.
It reassured her that
I was waiting on the beach.

I reminded her that, not far away, the sea was raging
with the violence of nature,
that the crashing waves on the rocks could be deadly.

"Yes," she replied, "something I have to see."

She had good reason to test the water,
to break the surface,
to see that I was standing calmly by.

I remembered what she said,
and did not take any notes any more.
As I said, this is a cautionary tale.

A Dialogue with Myself

How can Jungian psychology help me?

You mean, how can I use it to help myself?

No. I mean, in what way is Jungian psychology different?

Oh. In what specific ways might it help?

Yes. What's so great about it?

Nothing great. But it is a way of experiencing being.

I'm confused.

That is the beginning of everything.

Sounds like gibberish.

We have what we seek within us. One way to find it is through
analytical psychology.

As I said, how can Jungian psychology help me? Straight talk please!

It can be a point of reference
when life seems meaningless
and when self-doubt consumes you,
when suffering throttles you and
even pain is being,

when you are rootless and downhearted,
isolated from others,
preoccupied with yourself
and fear. . . .

**That sounds horrific. I am not so distraught. I just don't find life worthwhile . . .
anymore.**

So I have described you.
But you are living your personal life
in the timeless flow of all time and being.
Your history is beyond your personal life.

Beyond my personal life! You are not helping me at all.

Our quest is to understand and to become ourselves.
In that we become acquainted with our own myth,
our archetypal world in our collective unconscious.
Therein lie our own healing powers—our shadows.
There is "light at the core of darkness."

Not much clearer. What in the world are you saying?

I am saying:
Accept your immediate experience,
your dreams and your thoughts
as the source of your wholeness,
where you find yourself in your humanity.

My insurance company won't buy that.
Give me a DSM IIIR* diagnosis.

That's the point! You don't have a DSM IIIR diagnosis!
You do not have a *problem* to *solve*;
You have the predicament of life itself.
For that, your personal story is merely
the package in which you are.
When that "package" is opened,
your journey begins.
Your becoming becomes being.

Yeah! My becoming becomes my being!
Fat chance. Words, words, words. Fat words!

Yes, words, too, are only packaging.
They remain "fat words"
until the moment you discover meaning.
Most of our "story" is trivial
in the perspective of Being.

**Diagnostic Statistical Manual*, Third Revised Edition (American Psychiatric Association, 1987).

How do I know when the journey begins?

You know:
When you cease to blame anyone;
When you cease to reach too high;
When you cease to grasp and hold too much;
When you seek no name, no fame;
When being is belonging;
When belonging is where you are being;
When there is no self-object;
When there is no creed or doctrine;
When your dreams and fantasies speak to you;
When the innate language of your mind is talking;
When you listen without effort as natural as nature;
When risks are stepping stones;
When the irrational is the twin of reason;
When the insignificant is important.

Sounds too lofty, too off into ethereal thinking for me.
I want to set my feet firmly on the ground.
I want to live in reality, and do the work I can do and want to do.
I'd like to have enough money and just be happy.

There is no such thing as enough money.
You cannot be happy without also being unhappy.
If you float in exotic reverie of mandalas,
if you turn to the I Ching like breakfast cereal,
      then you mock Jung.
To find meaning means to be in the here and now;
      everyday life needs both light and darkness.

Well, I'll be damned . . . . If this is in *Understandable Jung*, then you're
speaking Greek.

Yes.
The descent to the underworld of the collective unconscious
was called the *Nekya* by the Greeks.
You can begin that journey alone.
If you feel compelled to go deeper and deeper,
then you need a guide.
If no such person is available to you,
you must do it as best as you can.
If you learn patience and cultivate equanimity,
you will find a great
Wisdom.
It was there all the time waiting to be found.

Me? Wisdom?

**   Maybe . . . . . . But I am beginning to learn that we can talk and talk forever, discuss and discuss ideas but if I don't experience these ideas in myself, the talk is all just gonna be a head trip. That is why I came to talk with you in the first place.**

When you leave, keep your head down
when you walk through the doorway.
Auf wiedersehn.

The Wise Old Man/The Wise Old Woman

Almost anyone who has heard of archetypes has heard of the Wise Old Man and the Wise Old Woman. In earliest life, our parents catch these projections. In maturity, we meet the archetype in others.

Jung said, "Together the patient and I address ourselves to the 2,000,000-year-old man that is in all of us. In the past analysis, most of our difficulties come from losing contact with our instincts, with the age-old unforgotten wisdom stored up in us. And where do we make contact with this old man in us? In our dreams. There are clear manifestations of our unconscious mind. They are the rendezvous of the racial history and of our current external problems" (McGuire and Hull 1977, p. 89).

The Wise Old Man archetype, for Jung, appeared as *Philemon,* with whom he had long conversations. "Philemon represented a force which was not myself. In my fantasies I had conversations with him, and he said things which I had not consciously thought. For I observed clearly that it was he who spoke, not I. . . . It was he who taught me psychic objectivity, the reality of the psyche. . . . Psychologically, Philemon represented superior insight. He was a mysterious figure to me. At times he seemed to me quite real, as if he were a living personality. I went walking up and down the garden with him, and to me, he was what the Indians call a guru" (1963, p. 183). This was Jung's most valued inner dialogue. You might imagine a theme song: "Me and My Daimonian Philemonian."

For many people, Jung himself carried the projection of the Wise Old Man. No doubt this gave him some pleasure as well as pain. Many women came to work and study with Jung, and to them, and to some men, he was a guru.

The shadow of the Wise Old Man/Woman is expressed in inflation and unquestioning belief in one's superiority and omniscience. When one begins to bow down to oneself, it is time to be ossified. In psychology, that somewhat airy subject, one may be the Wise Old One of Great Thoughts and Brilliant Interpretations and still be devoid of any wisdom of the common sense street smarts. To be an authentic Wise Old One, one may live in a cave or a golden pagoda, but must also dwell along the ordinary pathways, in ordinary cities, with ordinary people.

The Wise Old One has two principal characteristics: wisdom and humility.

Anyone who receives the projection of the Wise Old One archetype may also be perceived as a magician and carry an air of mystery. The shadow of the Wise Old One is the Old Fool.

Jung Catches Such a Projection

A friend of mine was profoundly affected when he read Jung's autobiography, *Memories, Dreams, Reflections.* He had a dream, which he wrote to me:

> *I meet Jung in his study in Kusnacht.*
> *We have a conversation.*
> *I ask him the big, meaning-of-life questions*
> *and he gives me vague answers.*
> *I get irritated.*
> *I accuse him of being a charlatan.*
> *He looks at me but says nothing in his defense.*
> *Instead, he grows an additional set of eyes*
> *above the set he normally sports.*
> *To this day I get chills up my spine*
> *when I recall the dream.*
> *Ah, wholeness!*

You know what Epictitus said? . . . "If you wish to make progress, you must be content in external matters to seem a fool and a simpleton; do not wish men to think you know anything, and if any should think you to be somebody, distrust yourself. For know that it is not easy to keep your will in accord with nature and to, at the same time, keep outward things; if you attend to one, you must needs neglect the other."

Do not wish women to think . . .
Why don't you speak for yourself?

EPILOGUE

Linoleum cut by Harry Wilmer

**The written word has meaning only
when actualized in life.**

Being

An interview: Hugh Downs and blind man.
Downs: "Have you been blind all your life?"
Blind man: "Not yet."

When you think about *Being,*
imagine the state of Being as accepting yourself
as you are, where you are, and when you are where you are.
Accepting and Being are what is.
Contrariwise, trying to relive the past
or live in a future in your mind
are not Being, there is no is-ness,
only "was," "will be," and "ought-to-be."

Reaching your possible some-better state of Being
is the nature of Becoming.
There is no Becoming, however, unless one comes from Being.
That is what Be-coming means.
All you have to be
is who you are at this instant,
accepting this as your present fate.

If you tell me
"where you are coming from"
by an endless recital of all the misfortunes
that you have suffered, and if it seems that you are
"crying over spilt milk,"
then I think that where you are coming from is:
The Archipelago of the Trivianas.
That is where the Straits of Spilt Milk
and the Shoals of Inconsequentia are to be found.
There blame is enthroned.

To want to Become all over again is dying, not living.
In Becoming, we are growing in relationship
to the outer world.
In Being, we are growing in relationship
to the inner world.
At the balanced existential junction, we are
being in *the* world.

Becoming is getting here.
Being is hereness.
Once you are truly Being,
you are not pushing for anything more;
you are not striving for name or fame.
You are in a state of equanimity
from which you can still become
what is in you to become.

That is the heart of contentment.
In your times of past Becomings,
you were many places to which you can never return.
If you dwell there in fantasy or obsession
you will be high, low,
or in limbo—
imprisoned by the Ifonlies.

Looking inward with your soul,
looking outward with your psyche,
at the point of interpenetration
of the spiritual and the material world,
you may see the essence of
Becoming and Being
breathing spirit.

Ultimately we realize
that this mysterious spirit
survives only in our daily chores
and in the ordinary work we do
in caring for ourselves and those entrusted to us.
Becoming and Being in the world we breathe.

Being and Becoming in the Here and Now

Do not declare war
    on yourself,
      nor on anyone else.
        No war.

Being in the here and now
is what is happening anyway.

Your collective unconscious,
can be a guide to inner peace.

Jung's words are not salvation,
but the richness of his thoughts
may help you to experience
the depth of your psyche, your soul.

Your dreams illuminate the way,
but live not in the dream.
Live in the here and now—
not in fantasy, but in the *hic et nunc.**
That is all there ever is
or was or will be.
This present moment,
like the river, is always changing,
never the river
it was when you saw it,
not ever.
It is always changing,
like you.

Before you can touch the river
that you saw, it is gone—
somewhere forever never ending,
always becoming the never present,
forever unending.

---

*Latin: "here and now"

The moment just passed and dead
is now this moment
that you are living.
And then it is gone and you are gone.*

Remember to forget
the past and don't forget
the remembered present.**
It is consciousness.

Remember that forgetting
is as close to happiness
as you will ever get because
there is one unchanging truth.
The only one there is:

This, Too, Shall Pass

      be it tragic,
      be it good,
      be it bad,
be it glory or defeat,
be it success or failure,
be it ennui or ecstasy,
be it fullness or emptiness—
      this, too, shall pass.

Winter becomes spring,
and spring summer,
and summer will become fall.
      It always has,
sure as the corn seed shall fall
giving birth
and growing into the earthy is-ness
of our bodies, minds, and souls.

Our fall is our rising up.
Our death is our birth.

---

*This poem was originally published, in a different version, in *The San Francisco Jung Institute Library Journal* (vol. 9, no. 3, 1990).
**Edelman, 1989.

Rejoice in
>   the cycle of creation,
>   the cycle of birth,
>   the cycle of death and rebirth.

The hope of the future . . .
this, too, shall pass in the coming present.

When the Lady comes walking,
and time comes stalking,
we shall sing "Hallelujah."

Gather ye faithful.
We shall remember you
>   as the one who
>   came from Mole Hill Mountain
>   on Big Deal Island.

When the Lady comes walking,
and time comes stalking,
we shall sing "Hallelujah"
to rejoice in this ramble, scramble creed:

>   Live for today.
>   Live just and only in the here and now.
>   Do not think that you *ought* to do anything.
>   Forget the past, remember the present.
>   Leave the future to itself.

Becoming

When we think of Being and Becoming—
the state of Being is to be
oneself as one is at the time Being.
In truly Being in the present,
we neither look to the past nor to the future.
There is no arrival and no departure.

There is just Being.
If we do not arrive, how do we get to Being?
We do not get there.
We Become there.
In Becoming who and what we are, where we are
now Being,
we have to have been Becoming.
Once Being there is no Becoming, no future.

No future? What do you mean, "No future?"
What if I am not satisfied with the present Being?
Is there *no* hope for a future?

That is all there is: *Hope* for the future.
It will be what it is to be when it is Being.
At that point, there will be *no* future all over again.
Once upon a time a futurologist-astrologer
published his *opus magnus* titled,
"How to Make the Future Work for Me."
It is available from Perpetua Ltd., Publishers.

In the first half of life, we are mainly Becoming.
In the second half of life, we are mostly Being.
To be always Becoming is to be always achieving and building.
Becoming is how you got here.
Being is where you are.
Being content there becomes you.
It is called inner growth.

In times of Becoming,
you were many places where you cannot go again.
Being content may not be Being satisfied,
but it is the way to be:
neither high nor low, but somewhere in between.
Becoming becomes Being becomes non-Being.

It is neither this nor that, yin nor yang, hot nor cold,
but thisthat, yinyang, hotcold,
masculinefeminine, femininemasculine, or bothand.

In Being without Becoming, we look inward—
not exactly a favorite American sport—
not exactly the outgoing, action-packed climber.
But it is Being alone *without* Being lonely.

OK! But sounds kinda loose to me. I don't get all this being/becoming mishmash. I'm from Missouri!

I am always Becoming older. See?
I know that because at any point of Being
I was always younger. OK? When Being stops, I am dead.
   Right?
When Becoming stops I am still an alive Being. Get it?

You are from Missouri, and I can only show you
who I am *here and now,* and that is all I am.

Why didn't you say that in the first place?

I'm from Schenectady.

Monsters enough
Without looking for them
While it seemed like we ran from this to that
We probably were standing more still
Than we thought.
Is there such a thing as *more still*
Short of rigor mortis
Or arguing whether your dogma
can beat my dogma?

Addendum: From a Medical Perspective

A Case of Thrombosis of the Jungian Artery

A middle-aged man suffering from the Midpoint of Life lived in a very strange complex. His sister, age twenty-five, lived in a modest duplex. To ensure professional confidence I will use the name Felix for this patient. For three years Felix had been in an Enantiodromial Malaise. His past history was uneventful.

His Angst was intense and on occasions when he attempted to eat his own shadow he became deathly ill and went downhill. Intense therapeutic efforts would revive him from a Complex Arrest.

He awoke at 3:00 a.m. one morning drenched in sweat, having had a horrendous nightmare which he refused to tell the doctor in the emergency room of the hospital. After heroic measures, he became calm and was admitted for observation. Extensive and expensive tests showed that he had Thrombosis of the Jungian Artery. This had resulted in an infarct of his Central Archetype which results, in 99% of the cases, in globus hystericus with the inability to swallow the shadow.

Clinical Evaluation

Chief Complaint: Inability to swallow the shadow
Diagnosis: Thrombosis of Jungian Artery
with infarct of the Central Archetype (the self)
Cause: Enantiodromial virus (airborne)
Secondary symptoms: Malaise, angst, nightmares,
and globus hystericus

Felix was ordered to submit to Jungian analysis by his diagnostician. At first he adamantly refused, maintaining that he had an inflammation of his alchemical tremendum and his coniunctionis was broken. However, he did agree to talk with an analyst who told him that the only known cure for Thrombosis of the Jungian Artery was Jungian analysis. He said he didn't believe in analysis.

This is a particularly difficult therapy because the Jungian artery bifurcates just before it enters the skull. The upper branch passes through inflation sulcus, and the lower branch passes through deflation gulch. Once the thrombosis evaporates in analysis, the Self heals and the shadow can be swallowed and digested.

The Course of the Jungian Analysis

Felix came to his first analytic hour with Great Trepidation, who sat patiently in the waiting room during the session. Felix sat in the chair and reminded the doctor that he had not come of his own volition. He was "ordered" to have a Jungian analysis. The analyst tried to show him the nuances of phrases by saying, "An ordered analysis is an oxymoron." This caused Felix to insist that he wanted an ordered analysis, which began with the telling of his dream of the previous night:

> *I am in a doctor's office. It looks nothing like this office, but resembled a medieval inquisitional torture chamber. I gasp and turn to see a huge black shadowy figure coming towards me.*
> *At this moment a deep voice says to me: "You must eat your shadow. You must swallow your shadow."*

I woke up shaking.

The analyst asked Felix what he thought the dream meant. He said the torture chamber was his angst, and the voice came from the shadowy figure behind him and would scare the thrombosis out of his Jungian artery. His analyst asked him if maybe, possibly, perhaps, the dark man might be a surgeon and this was an image of an operation in which he would be swallowed, i.e., rendered unconscious by anesthesia. Felix said, no, it couldn't be that.

They were at the fork in the artery already. From that point on, the analysis went smoothly for ten years. Then a strange thing happened. At 3:00 a.m. on the morning of the anniversary of the onset of his symptoms, he awoke cured and ran into the street shouting, "I can swallow my Shadow!" and "I can eat my shadow!" He was obviously individuating since his Jungian artery thrombosis had been dislodged. His neighbors were not enthralled.

Felix came for his next analytic hour, which would be his last one, and at the midpoint of the hour he suddenly recalled a dream he had the night before.

> *I am a Jungian analyst. My very first patient walks into my office and I can't see his or her face. Everything turns brilliantly white and a voice says, "You have met your Coincidentum Oppositorum and it is you!" At that point I realized that I had changed my mind about being an analyst.*

The analysis was terminated and Felix continued his successful work in the brokerage house of Lark, Park, and Kundalini. A two year follow-up revealed that he had had no more attacks of Thrombosis of the Jungian Artery, no more enantiodromial malaise, and he was eating shadow twice a day.

Bibliography

Achtemeier, P. J., ed. 1985. *Harper's Bible Dictionary*. San Francisco: Harper and Row.

Auden, W. H., and Kronenberger, L. 1962. *The Viking Book of Aphorisms*. New York: Viking Press.

Ayer, A. J. 1946. *Language, Truth & Logic*. New York: Dover Publications, Inc.

Barnaby, K., and D'Acierno, P., eds. 1990. *C. G. Jung and the Humanities: Toward a Hermeneutics of Culture*. Princeton, N.J.: Princeton University Press.

C. G. Jung: 1975. In *Pro-Helvetia*. Zurich, Switzerland: Department of Expositions, 1975.

Carroll, L. 1982. *Through the Looking Glass*. New York: Julian Messner.

Edelman, G. M. 1989. *The Remembered Present: A Biological Theory of Consciousness*. New York: Basic Books, Inc.

Emerson, R. W. 1841. The over-soul. In *The Harvard Classics*, edited by C. W. Eliot, vol. 5. New York: P. F. Collier and Sons, 1909.

Everly, L. 1963. *That Man Is You*. Toronto: Paulist Press.

Fenton, N., Riemer, E., and Wilmer, H., eds. 1967. *The Correctional Community: An Introduction*. Berkeley, Calif.: University of California Press.

Foote, S. 1854. *Quarterly Review* 95:516.

Hendricks, R. G. 1989. *Lao Tzu, Te Tao Chings*. New York: Ballantine Books.

Hesse, H. 1963. *Steppenwolf*. New York: Modern Library.

Hillman, J. 1991. The yellowing of the work. In *Personal and Archetypal Dynamics in the Analytical Relationship: Proceedings of the Eleventh International Congress for Analytical Psychology, Paris, 1989*, edited by M. A. Mattoon. Zurich: Daimon Verlag.

Hinsie, L. E., and Campbell, R. J. 1973. *Psychiatric Dictionary*. New York: Oxford University Press.

Hoffer, E. 1976. *In Our Time*. New York: Harper and Row.

Holmes, O. W. 1910. The chambered nautilus. In *The Harvard Classics*, vol. 3, edited by C. W. Eliot. New York: P. F. Collier & Son.

Jung, C. G. 1921. *Psychological Types. CW*, vol. 6. Princeton, N.J.: Princeton University Press, 1971.

_____. 1932. Psychotherapists or the clergy. In *CW* 11:327-347. Princeton, N.J.: Princeton University Press, 1969.

_____. 1934. The meaning of psychology for modern man. In *CW* 10: 134-156. Princeton, N.J.: Princeton University Press, 1964.

_____. 1935. The Tavistock Lectures. *CW* 18: 1-182. Princeton, N.J.: Princeton University Press, 1976.

_____. 1943. The psychology of the unconscious. In *CW* 7:3-119. Princeton, N.J.: Princeton University Press, 1953.

_____. 1944. *Psychology and Alchemy. CW*, vol. 12. Princeton, N.J.: Princeton University Press, 1953.

_____. 1946. *Letters,* edited by G. Adler, vol. 1. Princeton, N.J.: Princeton University Press, 1975.

_____. 1948a. General aspects of dream psychology. *CW* 8:237-280. Princeton, N.J.: Princeton University Press, 1969.

_____.1948b. On the nature of dreams. *CW* 8:281-298. Princeton, N.J.: Princeton University Press, 1969.

_____. 1951. The psychology of the child archetype. In *CW* 9i: 151-181. Princeton, N.J.: Princeton University Press, 1959.

_____. 1951b. Fundamental questions of psychotherapy. In *CW,* 16:111-125. Princeton, N.J.: Princeton University Press, 1966.

_____. 1954a. Transformation symbolism in the mass. In *CW* 11:201-296. Princeton, N.J.: Princeton University Press, 1958.

_____. 1954b. Archetypes of the collective unconscious. In *CW* 9i:3-41. Princeton, N.J.: Princeton University Press, 1959.

_____. 1955. *Letters,* edited by G. Adler, vol. 2. Princeton, N.J.: Princeton University Press, 1975.

_____. 1957. Commentary of "The Secret of the Golden Flower." In *CW* 13:1-55. Princeton, N.J.: Princeton University Press, 1967.

_____. 1958. *Letters,* edited by G. Adler, vol. 2. Princeton, N.J.: Princeton University Press, 1975.

_____. 1959. *Letters,* edited by G. Adler, vol. 2. Princeton, N.J.: Princeton University Press, 1975.

_____. 1960. *Letters,* edited by G. Adler, vol. 2. Princeton, N.J.: Princeton University Press, 1975.

_____. 1961. Symbols and the interpretations of dreams. In *CW* 18:183-265. Princeton, N.J.: Princeton University Press, 1976.

_____. 1963. *Memories, Dreams, Reflections,* edited by Aniela Jaffe. New York: Pantheon Books.

_____. 1978. *Psychological Reflections: A New Anthology of His Writings,* edited by Jolande Jacobi. Princeton, N.J.: Princeton University Press.

McGuire, W., and Hull, R. C., eds. 1977. *C. G. Jung Speaking: Interviews and Encounters.* Princeton, N.J.: Princeton University Press.

Pribram, K. H. 1991. *Brain and Perception: Holonomy and Structure in Figural Processing.* Hillside, N.J.: Lawrence Erlbaum Associates.

Samuels, A. 1990. Beyond the feminine principle. In *C. G. Jung and the Humanities: Toward a Hermeneutics of Culture,* edited by K. Barnaby and P. D'Acierne. Princeton, N.J.: Princeton University Press.

Snow, C. P. 1959. *The Two Cultures and the Scientific Revolution.* Cambridge, Mass.: Cambridge University Press.

Suzuki, D. T. 1961. *Essays in Zen Buddhism,* first series. New York: Grove Press, Inc.

_____. 1972. *What Is Zen?* New York: Harper and Row.

Thompson, D. W. 1942. *Growth and Form.* Cambridge, Mass.: Cambridge University Press.

Tucker, E. 1980. Voices from the silents. *The Quarterly Journal of the Library of Congress* 37:387.

Ullman, M. 1988. The experiential dream group. In *The Variety of Dream Experience,* edited by M. Ullman and C. Limmer. New York: Continuum.

Valery, P. 1894. The method of Leonardo. In *Paul Valery: An Anthology,* edited by J. R. Lawler. Princeton, N.J.: Princeton University Press, 1977.

van der Post, L. 1975. *Jung and the Story of Our Time.* New York: Pantheon Books.

Veninga, J., and Wilmer, H., eds. 1985. *Vietnam in Remission.* College Station, Tx.: Texas A&M University Press.

Wilber, Ken, ed. 1982. *The Holographic Paradigm and Other Paradoxes.* Boston: Shambhala.

Wilmer, H. 1941. *Huber the Tuber: The Lives and Loves of a Tubercle Bacillus.* New York: American Tuberculosis Association.

_____. 1958. *Social Psychiatry in Action.* Springfield, Ill.: Charles C. Thomas Publisher.

_____. 1964. A living group experiment at San Quentin prison. *Corrective Psychiatry and Journal of Social Therapy* 10:80-91.

_____. 1965. The role of the rat in prison. *Federal Probation* 29:44-49.

_____. 1968. Innovative uses of videotape on a psychiatric ward. *Hospital and Community Psychiatry* 19:119-123.

_____. 1968b. Television as Participant Observer. *American Journal of Psychiatry* 124:3-11.

————. 1969. Drugs, hippies, and doctors. *Journal American Medical Association* 206:1272-1275.

————. 1982. Dream seminar for chronic schizophrenic patients. *Psychiatry* 45:351-360.

————. 1986. The healing nightmare: A study of war dreams of Vietnam combat veterans. *Quadrant*, 19(1):47-62.

————. 1992. Dreams of an analysand dying of AIDS. In *Closeness in Personal and Professional Relationships*, edited by H. Wilmer. Boston: Shambhala Publications, Inc.

Wilmer, H., Marks, I., and Pogue, E. 1966. Group treatment of prisoners and their families. *Mental Hygiene* 50:380-389.

Welch, H. 1966. *Taoism: The Parting of the Way*. Boston: Beacon Press.

Chiron Publications thanks the following for their permission.

Page
ii   Photo reprinted by permission of Guido Cerf.
Jung, Carl Gustav; C. G. JUNG LETTERS. Copyright © 1975 by Princeton University Press. Reprinted by permission of Princeton University Press.

1   Photo copyright © by Universal City Studios, Inc. Reprinted courtesy of MCA Publishing Rights, a Division of MCA, Inc.

3   Photos used courtesy of the author.

10   Jung, Carl Gustav; C. G. JUNG LETTERS. Copyright © 1975 by Princeton University Press. Reprinted by permission of Princeton University Press.

44   Photo reprinted by permission from *Hospital and Community Psychiatry*.

45-46   Photos used courtesy of the author.

51   Reprinted by permssion from Dover Publications, Inc.

89   Jung, Carl Gustav; COLLECTED WORKS, vol. 10, second edition. Copyright © 1970 by Princeton University Press. Reprinted by permission of Princeton University Press.

104   Jung, Carl Gustav; COLLECTED WORKS, vol. 8, second edition. Copyright © 1969 by Princeton University Press. Reprinted by permission of Princeton University Press.
Jung, Carl Gustav; COLLECTED WORKS, vol. 18. Copyright © 1976 by Princeton University Press. Reprinted by permission of Princeton University Press.

110   Jung, Carl Gustav; COLLECTED WORKS, vol. 18. Copyright © 1976 by Princeton University Press. Reprinted by permission of Princeton University Press.

149   Reprinted from STEPPENWOLF by Hermann Hesse (New York: Modern Library, 1963), pp. 33-34. Permission sought from Harcourt Brace Inc.

154   Jung, Carl Gustav; COLLECTED WORKS, vol. 11, second edition. Copyright © 1969 by Princeton University Press. Reprinted by permission of Princeton University Press.

174   Jung, Carl Gustav; COLLECTED WORKS, vol. 13. Copyright © 1969 by Princeton University Press. Reprinted by permission of Princeton University Press.

175   Jung, Carl Gustav; COLLECTED WORKS, vol. 11, second edition. Copyright © 1969 by Princeton University Press. Reprinted by permission of Princeton University Press.

200   Jung, Carl Gustav; COLLECTED WORKS, vol. 9, part 1, second edition. Copyright © 1969 by Princeton University Press. Reprinted by permission of Princeton University Press.

221   Jung, Carl Gustav; C. G. JUNG LETTERS. Copyright © 1975 by Princeton University Press. Reprinted by permission of Princeton University Press.

228   Photo reprinted by permission of Verkehrsrerein der Stadt Bern, Switzerland.

233   Jung, Carl Gustav; COLLECTED WORKS, vol. 16, second edition. Copyright © 1966 by Princeton University Press. Reprinted by permission of Princeton University Press.

248   Paul Kaufman, personal communication used with permission.

Index